AMERICAN INDIAN ANTIQUES

Arts and Artifacts of the Northeast

Chief Red Cloud - Cayuga

AMERICAN INDIAN ANTIQUES

Arts and Artifacts of the Northeast

Virginia Vidler

SOUTH BRUNSWICK AND NEW YORK: A. S. BARNES AND COMPANY
LONDON: THOMAS YOSELOFF LTD

A. S. Barnes and Co., Inc.
Cranbury, New Jersey 08512

Thomas Yoseloff Ltd
108 New Bond Street
London W1Y OQX, England

Library of Congress Cataloging in Publication Data

Vidler, Virginia, 1928-
  American Indian antiques.

  Bibliography: p.
  Includes index.
  1. Indians of North America—Culture. 2. Indians of North America—Imple-
ments. 3. Antiques—United States. I. Title.
E78.E2V52 1975   974'.004'97   74-9302
ISBN 0-498-01495-9

PRINTED IN THE UNITED STATES OF AMERICA

IN MEMORIAM

To Charles A. Neumann, *Ha-nah-dia-shu* ("Keeper of the Hill"), a good person and a good friend who generously shared with us his lifetime collections, remembrances, and appreciation of Woodland Indian ways

CONTENTS

ACKNOWLEDGMENTS

It's people who make an undertaking such as this possible. I want to thank the many friends and new-found acquaintances who opened their homes, historical museums, private collections, scrapbooks, and memories to me.

Twylah Hurd Nitsch is a repositor of the ancient Seneca wisdom taught her by her grandfather, Moses Shongo, a medicine doctor and philosopher, who through his formal education was able to see and interpret the ancient Indian philosophies for contemporary times. In friendship she shared with me much knowledge of the People of Wisdom through courses at Rosary Hill College Human Dimensions Institute in Buffalo, New York and afforded me access to the Shongo-Hurd Collection.

My two friends, Beverly F. Stoughton and Janice Mogavero, gave me much professional help without which this manuscript would not have been published.

Mr. and Mrs. Lewellyn Casterline, Mrs. Laura Neumann, Mr. and Mrs. Arthur Werner, and Dr. Virginia Cummings, Director of the Buffalo Museum of Science, all added their knowledge, background experiences, and collections to give the personal touches necessary for such a book.

Mr. John Ritch spent a day with me while I photographed collections in the Natural History Building at the Smithsonian Institution in Washington D. C.

Mr. Richard Hill of the Buffalo and Erie County Historical Society gave me a great deal of time and consultation on technical details.

Mr. Keith Lickers, former Director of the Woodland Cultural-Education Centre in Brantford, Ontario, Canada was most helpful.

Mrs. Andrea Shaw, Director of Old Amherst Colony Museum, Amherst, New York gave us access to photograph the Charles Neumann Collection now housed there.

My deepest appreciation to my husband, Edward, who added two vital ingredients to this project: pictures and patience!

Friend and artist, Rix Jennings, created the jacket and interior drawings to enhance the work.

Other museums where collections aided my research include: The Museum of the American Indian Heye Foundation in New York City; the Indian Trade Room at Old Fort Niagara in Lewiston, New York; the Concord Historical Society in Springville, New York, that houses the Pop Warner Collection, and the Holland Purchase Historical Society in Batavia, New York.

My thanks also to the ever-patient librarians of the large city museums who helped with their excellent research talents and particularly to Mrs. Betty Cook of our Town of Aurora Library. The assistance of these unsung heroes proved invaluable.

To all of you. . . . Nyah-Weh ("thank you!").

INTRODUCTION

What could be more precious in American antiques than the wares of the only people in this country whose ancestry predates, by thousands of years, the arrival of Columbus?

"Indian antiques? Don't you mean relics?" No. Leave behind those well-documented objects that rest in museum archives. Move forward to about 1760, just before the American Revolutionary war. This period, referred to by museologists as contemporary, is recognized by the antiques collector as the period providing some of the most rare and sought after of pre-American antiques.

Indian antiques may be defined as the ancestral possessions of today's native American Indian. Surely, these contributions should be catalogued for our bookshelves along with those of the Colonists, Shakers, Pennsylvania Dutch, and many other people who added their cultures to the antique heritage in America. These are the items that were made when the last traces of the old ways were torn away and Northeastern American Indians found themselves walking, as they say, "with one foot in a moccasin and the other in a shoe."

Although their designs were influenced by decades of change and white man's tastes, there remains a fascination in Northeastern American Indian antiques. They still reveal fine craftsmanship and a feeling of mythology, symbolism, and living in harmony with nature.

Owners of historical Indian objects have constant difficulty in identifying those Indian things which originated from this northeastern section of America. When these items are sought at shows, estate auctions, flea markets, and antique shops, dealers often remark, "I don't know exactly what they made around here." Many people are familiar with the war bonnet and spear images of Hollywood and television Indians. They tend to brand everything as Indian, while actually they are recalling the styles and motifs of plains and western Indians who, over the years, were so publicized and exploited commercially.

Our Northeastern Indians, already in their period of demise when the first wagons rolled Westward ho, left their wares and precious belongings behind just as other early Americans did. These Northeastern American Indian antiques are becoming more valuable than any others. Early in the century, when these objects were actively collected, they ran the gamut from rare to fairly common. Today, because they are so in demand, prices are soaring and you may unknowingly own some rare pieces. Without proper identification they are valueless, but with it they become almost priceless. This is the time to dust them off, identify, and display them with pride!

In order to identify and date Indian possessions, it's necessary to be aware of the changes that influenced the Indians' life styles. Often this dating can only be general; however, there are three broad workable periods of time into which Indian antiques from the Northeast can be classified.

1. The pre-Revolutionary war period from about 1760 to 1776 includes items of ceremonial, tribal, personal, and trade use that reflect Indian life at that time. Early settlers, upon arriving on the East Coast, were fascinated by their friendly encounters with Indians. They traded eagerly for Indian goods and the Indians were just as anxious for theirs. Antique acquisitions from this period are rare, very expensive, and turn up unexpectedly. That's why it's important to know them when you see them.

2. The post-Revolutionary war period from 1776 to 1800. These were decades of turmoil and confusion during which there was a displacement of possessions in both directions. Indians were grabbing white men's things and whites were grabbing those of the Indians. There was much bartering because few people had cash. Indian items from this period are rare and expensive, but they are occasionally available.

3. The Reservation period from 1800 to the early 1900s. The first half of this century was characterized by the almost complete cultural expiration of the American Indian. Poverty, alcoholism and indifference had set in; sacred family possessions were sold by Indian families or stolen from them. After 1860, many good things were made on the reservations specifically for sale to outsiders. They were designed to please white men.

Some readers will recall seeing Indians selling handmade items on city streets and at country fairs fifty or sixty years ago. They came from nearby reservations with model-T truck loads of bent willow furniture, beaded necklaces, belts, arm bands, pin cushions, leather work, moccasins, and hand-hammered jewelry. Those items, purchased for dimes and quarters, sifted into attics, trunks, boxes, and bookcases throughout the Northeast. Families, now realizing that they own some old Indian pieces, are surprised to find that these are real treasures dating from the 1920s or 1930s. During that same period, perceptive Indian collectors recognized that these items might become a lost art. They accumulated whole collections from specific Northeastern tribes and reservations and were interested enough to record the details of their collections from these three periods of time. Forty years ago, antique dealers were glad for the few customers who collected Indian things. There weren't many outlets for them. For decades since then, many of those antiques were pushed aside, neglected and gathering dust.

Today, antique collectors are thrilled to recognize a mask or to use a beaded sash for a wall hanging; to identify and wear a silver brooch, an intriguing environmental stone; or, perhaps, to display a wooden corn soup bowl on an end table. Authorities agree that there is a renaissance in all things Indian.

AMERICAN INDIAN ANTIQUES

Arts and Artifacts of the Northeast

1

MEET THE WOODLANDERS

IMAGINE the white men's surprise when they were greeted by Indians wearing European broadcloth clothes, silver jewelry, and carrying brass-tipped arrows! Originally, trading had begun before the Pilgrims' arrival on the North American continent.

These Indians of the Northeast are known as Woodland Indians of the North. There was a mutual fascination between newly arriving Europeans and the Indians who were often described in journals as the most noble appearing of men. They were of Algonquian and Iroquoian blood lines with dozens of tribes and nations listed under each of these headings. Taking quickly to European ways and goods, the native Americans were eager to adapt white men's clothing, tools, weapons, and household utensils for their own use. Years later, this copying and adapting would cause researchers to devote much study to the influences of Scotch, French, English, Pioneer, Quaker, and Shaker designs on the items made by Indians in the Northeastern section of America.

It's difficult to designate by states the areas in which these Indians originated. After all, the sur-

veyors' lines came centuries after Indian trails had been worn deep into the earth's surface. By 1760, most pure traces of individual Woodland tribes or their original culture areas were long gone. Thousands of people had been uprooted and reduced by wars and disease to groups numbering in the hundreds. Many individual tribes were now blended into general groups.

The five Iroquois nations of New York State remained united and strong in influence until the American Revolutionary War. Strategically located, they held the key position to the eastern Great Lakes and the land through which much of the war travel took place. They received great attention. Silver, weapons, and other gifts of white men were heaped upon them as the French, English, and Colonists vied for their support. The tastes of the Iroquois became very selective when it came to gifts. They also dominated the Delaware Indians of New Jersey, Ohio, and Pennsylvania. After the Revolutionary war, those Iroquois who were pro-English (led by Joseph Brant) were given refuge at the Brant Reservation in Ontario, Canada and still

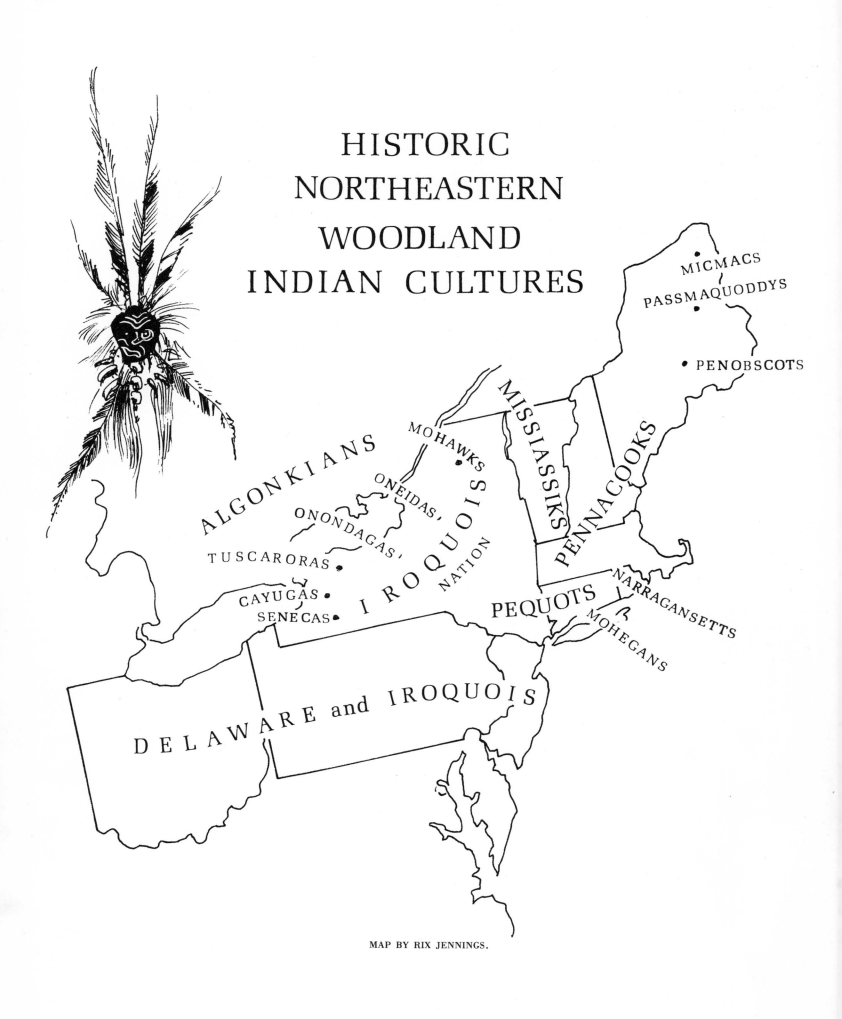

HISTORIC NORTHEASTERN WOODLAND INDIAN CULTURES

MICMACS

PASSMAQUODDYS

PENOBSCOTS

ALGONKIANS

MOHAWKS

MISSIASSIKS

PENNACOOKS

ONEIDAS,

ONONDAGAS,

TUSCARORAS

IROQUOIS

NATION

CAYUGAS

SENECAS

PEQUOTS

NARRAGANSETTS

MOHEGANS

DELAWARE and IROQUOIS

MAP BY RIX JENNINGS.

retain their Iroquoian identity today. Others had tried in vain to remain neutral and were caught in the wake of the American Revolution. Their crops and homes were destroyed.

Compared to the Iroquois, New England Indians made a rather insignificant contribution to the antiques of this period from 1760 to 1900. Caught between the French and English in the early colonization of New England, these Indians could not avoid the crush of white civilization. Known originally as Abenakis, Merrimacs, Pequots, Narragansetts, and Mohegans,

their true identity would be traced for them in white men's history books decades later. It was easier, by Revolutionary war time, to refer to them as Atlantic Seacoast Indians.

After the Revolution, there would be no reconstruction period for Northeastern Indians. White man's attention was now moving to the Indian lands of the West. Our Northeastern Woodland Indians were soon to be forgotten on scrublands in the wilderness called reservations. They would not be discovered again until the decades of the 1960s and 1970s.

2

DESIGNS FROM NATURE

INDIANS put decorations on all of their clothing, ceremonial costumes, and personal items such as pipe stems, knife holders, pouches, and moccasins. There's no mistaking Indian designs for anything else, but it's easier to call an item just "Indian" without giving it proper geographic identification.

A trained eye will see that the Woodland Indian antiques are distinctive and entirely different in beaded designs from the geometric-animalistic motifs associated with Indians of the plains and West. The reason for this is that the ancestors of Woodland Indians were not migratory compared to the hunters of the West. Although their villages had to be relocated every ten or fifteen years when the land became exhausted and game scarce, Woodland Indians lived in the same general areas for generation upon generations.

Think nature and you'll appreciate that the designs of Indians from this section of the country tell of their love for the forests where their ancestors once roamed free. Trees, flowers, sun, moon, sky, rivers —all are delicately and painstakingly recorded in repeated patterns that circle, swirl, and arc.

Originally, rich earth and dense forests provided game, berries, abundant crops, and a good life. Fast waterways and river systems made canoe travel easy. Men of the tribes were often gone whole seasons at a time visiting villages hundreds of miles away. Their women stayed behind to do the planting, harvesting, and food preparation. There were long hours by the fires and quiet winter seasons. They had time to develop their arts and crafts. Originally, they used quill, moosehair, small seeds, and tiny stone embroidery designs. Since there was no written language, their life philosophies were passed from mothers to daughters through embroidery designs, and their tribal secrets through the men's wood carvings. Wampum belts and strings were used to convey messages and agreements and to record history.

Eventually porcupine quills and moosehair gave way to beads introduced by traders. A few Indian artisans retained the old crafts from generation to

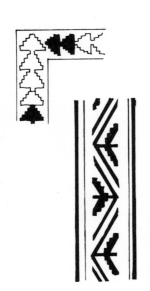
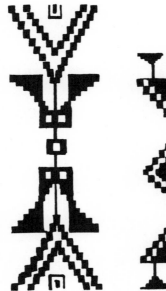

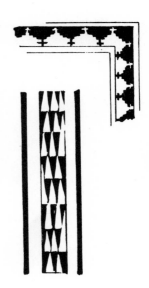

Art designs of Northeastern Indians are strikingly different from those of the West. The top three drawings are Woodland motifs that show the use of circles, swirls, arcs, flowers, and lacy patterns as compared to the bottom row of Western Indian designs that are done in straight lines that have a geometric appearance. DRAWING BY RIX JENNINGS

generation, but it became easier to trade for glass beads than to obtain quills. As generations passed, outside teachings by missionaries and new materials and tools began to affect beaded embroidery designs. The size of the beads and manner in which they were applied help to date these items. Many Indian motifs trace back to French religious vestments in embroidery designs. The use of thread and needles on cloth, instead of on skin, allowed new expressions in embroidery. Elaborate designs became possible and the simple, older symbols changed as a result of white contacts. Each Indian began creating her own designs in fruits and flowers. Border patterns of fine white beads on dark cloth were popular by 1760. Ribbon applique was also blind-stitched to the edge of garments as a background for beadwork. Designs varied from straight rows of tiny seed beads to lacy patterns, circles, and scrolls. By 1860, heavy embossed (raised) designs in larger colored beads came into style. Much beadwork was accumulated

from this era because it appealed to the tastes of white homemakers. Often, in the early 1900s, a collector could shop for beaded objects distinctive of a well-known Indian woman artisan on a particular reservation. Also, by 1900, Northeastern Indian beadwork had moved into the Victorian era. Large opaque or pearl-colored beads were strung on thread and stitched to the objects in elaborate designs of flowers. The sewing machine had now been introduced and was often used to stitch the side seams of objects. Indians in this section of the country now realized that their sales could be increased by copying the popular, better-known geometric designs used by Western Indians. Head, armbands, and necklaces done in Western motifs were added to their lines for sale to whites. These were done in tiny colored seed beads much the same as those done in present-day bead crafts. Commercialization had set in.

However, beaded items made for sale and those made for personal use were two different matters.

This Delaware pouch, about 1850, beautifully illustrates Woodland Indian designs. It is made of black velvet, edged with red cloth, and solidly beaded on front and back with tiny seed beads. Men's pouches like this were worn to ceremonies to hold pipes and tobacco. COURTESY OF THE SMITHSONIAN INSTITUTION.

This rare antique, almost two hundred years old and in perfect condition, was made with tiny glass beads on maroon cloth. It is labeled "a lambrequin," which was a border decoration hung from the edge of a plate rail or used as a valance on a window. This adaptation of a French idea was perhaps made on request. COURTESY OF THE POP WARNER COLLECTION.

This purse flap, dating about 1875, was lined with a page from a Bible printed in the Mohawk Indian language. COURTESY OF IROQRAFTS LTD., OHSWEKEN, ONTARIO.

A disassembled pouch with round beads and design applied in a flat effect date it about 1875. Considered in very good condition, the pouch was priced at thirty-five dollars. COURTESY OF IROQRAFTS, LTD., OHSWEKEN, ONTARIO.

The heavy raised embossing on this pair of cuffs, priced at sixty dollars, was typical of Northeastern Canadian beadwork in the early 1900s. COURTESY OF IROQRAFTS, LTD., OHSWEKEN, ON-TARIO.

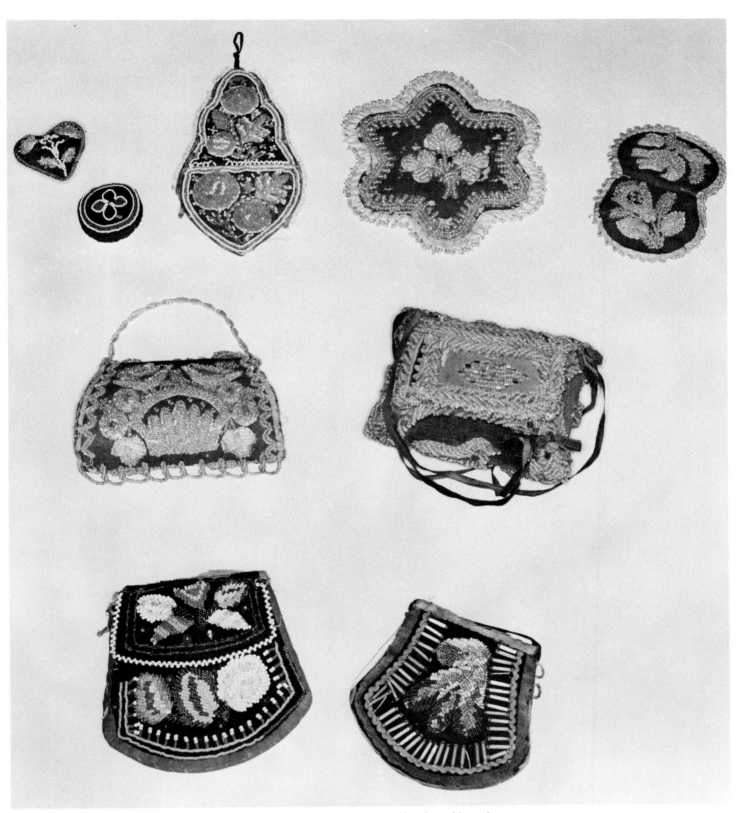

This array shows the changes in types of beads and how they were applied. The two purses (bottom row), dating about 1850, illustrate typical Woodland motifs. Those in the middle row are heavily embossed with clear beads, have less definition in design, indicating the change to Victorian tastes by the 1890s. The top row (left to right) has artistic beadwork on pin cushions, a hanging wall pocket for matches, a table mat, and a sewing-needle holder, from early 1900s.

Even though the designs were transformed by centuries of change, some fine aesthetic beaded items were made for personal use. Trees still figured prominently in these, as well as fruits, flowers, and sky domes resting on parallel lines that represented earth.

Many people are not aware of the quantities and varieties of purses, pouches, pin cushions, belts, arm bands, and novelty items produced during the Reservation period. For example, many novelty items were made at that time for the Niagara Falls tourist trade.

Recently, a beaded chicken sold for two dollars in an antique shop in western New York. The clear beads and their size date the item from about 1890, the Reservation period. The seller, not recognizing the true origin of the beaded work, didn't think it was Indian —just old. Its fragile appearance and dust made it dull looking. When dish-detergent suds were applied to the beads with a soft brush, they cleaned up nicely; and in spite of a few moth holes, the owner has it proudly on display. The words, "From Niagara Falls," awkwardly formed in white seed beads across the wide flat tail, cause one to wonder if the maker had ever enjoyed the opportunity to visit this world-famous tourist attraction.

The pin cushion on the left had the old, flat Iroquoian beadwork done in fine details. The souvenir purse from Niagara Falls had embossed designs done in clear glass beads. These two sales items reflect the change in beadwork that began in the late Reservation period.

Novelty items dating from 1875 to 1915 and typical of the Victorian era for which they were made to sell were: (bottom, left to right) a table mat and child's purse; (middle) a pin cushion; (top row, left to right) a four-cornered purse and a man's watch case. Designs were drawn on a piece of brown paper bag that was then tacked to the flat piece of material with thread and needle and the beads applied on top. COURTESY OF THE POP WARNER COLLECTION.

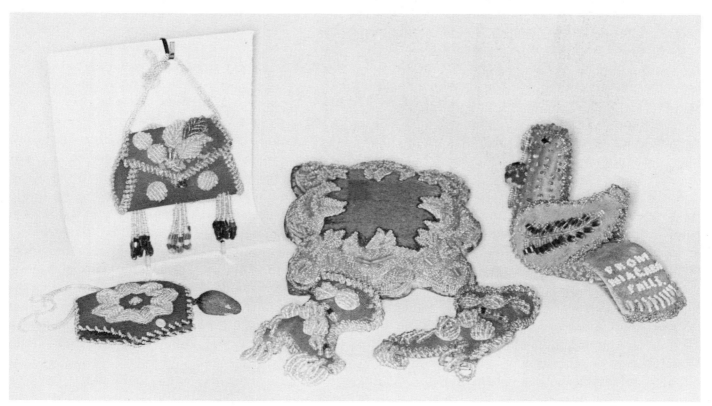

A common variety of late Reservation period novelty items found at shows, flea markets, and household sales in 1973–1974, ranged in price from one dollar to eight dollars.

3

MASKS AND MYTHS

MASKS, among the most coveted possessions in Indian collections, seem to convey all the qualities of excitement, mystery, wonder, and symbolism associated with Indian lore. Ceremonial masks were handed down in Indian families from generation to generation, as were the daguerreotypes and family Bibles of white men. For this reason, one doesn't happen upon a ceremonial mask in an antique shop or at a flea market. Occasionally, collectors who knew how to go about it could have a mask carved. Otherwise, it took time and patience to track one down, to prove a sincere interest, and then convince an owner to sell.

The Iroquois tribes of New York were regarded as the greatest of mask makers. Their masks, made of basswood, cedar, cucumber wood, pine, or corn husks are distinctive. They can be identified easily by the humanlike appearances. Whether laughing, crying, witless, crooked-nosed, or hang-lipped, the solid wooden faces were clearly intended to be artistic interpretations of human emotions and spiritual power. They are entirely different from Western Indian masks that resemble totem-pole-type faces of animals, birds, and nonhuman heads.

For thousands of years, the Iroquois Indians have considered life an inner struggle between light and dark, good and bad. Ancient legends tell that the False Faces live on the rocky-world rim. In the morning their faces are red and in the afternoon black as they follow the sun's path. Therefore, masks carved before noon were painted red; those at noon divided in red and black, and those after noon, black.

The wearer of a false face wasn't really trying to hide his identity, but to symbolize an emotion. He was described in diaries of white men as cavorting about the tribal fire dancing, chanting, and going into a trance. All of the rituals, the dances, songs, masks, and paraphernalia associated with the Indian way of life were interpreted and chronicled for texts by white men, often incorrectly. Twylah Hurd Nitsch suggests in her teaching that it was white man, upon seeing the Indian's arms outstretched to the sun, who called him a sun worshipper. The Indian was really giving thanks for another day. He believed that spiritual light

Medicine Mask from the early Reservation Period.

Male and female corn-husk masks. COURTESY OF THE NEUMANN COLLECTION.

dwelled within each person; that you have to know yourself before you can communicate with others. The False Face Society was originally an organization of philosophers. Over the years it took on sorcery, witchcraft, and demons through white men who told Indians they were pagans and would be punished. Naturally, with all that was happening around them, the Indians were willing to try anything to appease anyone's god.

Wooden masks, used by secret societies in each village, were symbolic representations in both religious and medicine ceremonies and at festivals.

They were not worshipped. Each one was carved from a living tree in order to pass energy into the masks. Bags of tobacco tied in the rear were tokens of gratitude. Tobacco was considered to have power similar to church incense of whites. The human hair on a mask was often that of a long deceased clan (family group) mother. It might seem a strange custom unless you stop to think of Victorian hair jewelry and mourning pictures done in human hair. Many people have their grandmothers' hair packed away in attic trunks. Placing the hair on a ceremonial mask seemed meaningful to Iroquois Indians.

*Spoon Mouth with no teeth. Spires on forehead are symbolic of a
snapping turtle's tail. According to Iroquoian cosmology, the earth
rests on a giant snapping turtle's back.*

Spoon Mouth with teeth. Is there anyone who has not had his mouth feel like the one on this old medicine ceremony mask looks?
COURTESY OF THE NEUMANN COLLECTION.

Beggar mask.

Another version of a Beggar mask, carved in the late 1800s.

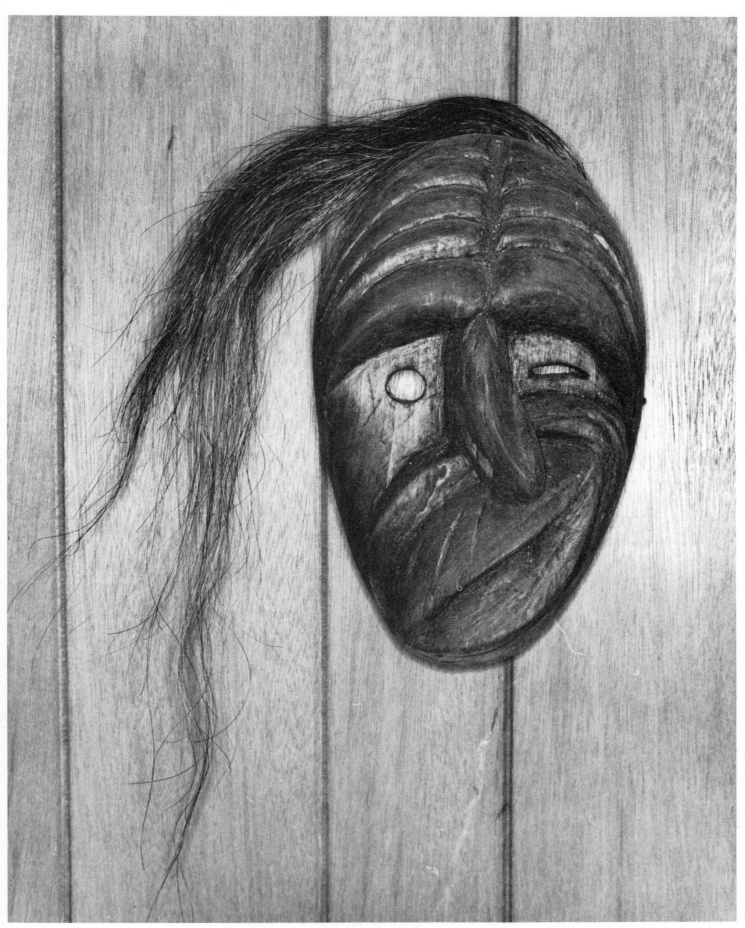

Old Broken Nose Mask from the early Reservation period.

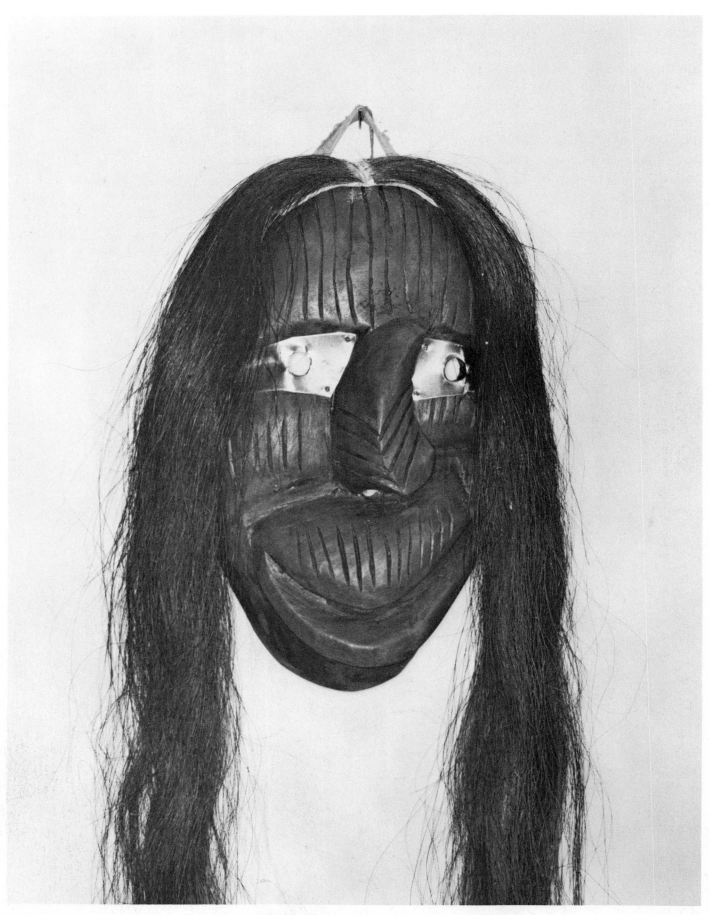

Contemporary Broken Nose mask that shows the difference in rendition.

Contortions on mask faces signified the role performed in a medicine healing ceremony. Other face designs clearly indicated physical and psychological problems; still others were portraitlike representations of people with whom Indians had contact outside their own villages. For instance, some masks had Oriental features. Although often noted as seeking favors from the gods, beggar masks were really used in humor to evoke laughter from the audience at ceremonies. Indians loved humor and beggar masks were objects of jest and happiness.

The exact legends of face details became obscured by hundreds of years of time. A carver did not hesitate to copy another nation's face designs if he learned that a certain mask had helped someone else. Thus, there is a linking and similarity of designs in masks among Indians of the entire Northeast. Women did not perform mask ceremonies but could be members of the False Face Society if a mask had helped them.

Early wooden masks are recognizable by their simplicity in workmanship. They were roughly carved; had features detailed in red, black, or white colors made from earth dyes; and were decorated with clam shells and long stringy human hair or hair made from basswood bark. When metal knives became available, mask makers were able to be more elaborate in carving facial features. They switched to barn paints, sheet copper, and horsetail hair obtained in trading. Masks made after 1760 are very stylized in rendition. Old Broken Nose was the first of the symbolic Iroquoian face types. Legend relates that his nose was broken and mouth twisted in a contest of power with the Creator. Because he demonstrated great strength, Old Broken Nose assumed the role of a doorkeeper in

Corn-husk mask. COURTESY OF THE NEUMANN COLLECTION.

This very old corn-husk mask has a definite personality! Collectors find that they all do.

the lives of Iroquois. Even today, he hangs near the doors of Indian lodges or homes to ward off bad luck.

Masks are still carved and sold, not for ceremonial purposes, but more as art objects with portraitlike qualities. Some of these modern masks have turned up deliberately distressed and resold as antiques. Because of this, modern mask carvers from the Iroquois Nation are numbering and recording mask sales to prevent them from being sold as antiques with price tags of three hundred dollars and up. New masks are light in weight, more detailed in features, and the hair is glued on the top instead of being strung through holes in the back as old ones were done.

Corn-husk masks were made only by the Iroquois. They represent ideas entirely different from the wooden-faced masks and should not be thought of in the same category. They relate to much happiness — planting, harvesting, feasts, and nature. They were used to give thanks for the abundance of agriculture. They were made of braided or twined strips of corn husk that were coiled around and around and held in place with husk fiber or twine. The fringed edges give these masks a sunburst quality. While one seems to look like another, they are actually done in dozens of designs. Here again, white men affixed names to these designs —cornflower, bisexual, disappearing image, and old man. Female masks were worn by women and male by men in order that the masks would symbolize the proper sex. There was festivity associated with these masks. They were used at New Year, midwinter, green-corn planting, and other agricultural ceremonies. Husk maskers appeared at ceremonies as symbols of the harvest and performed a dance using digging sticks and hoes to inaugurate the planting season. Although usually considered a woman's craft, anyone could make a corn-husk mask. They were very

popular items in 1900–1925, the peak era for Reservation period sale items. Many are in museums, historical society collections, and private ownership.

Miniature masks, less than three inches in diameter, are still somewhat mysterious. Those who know about them keep the real meaning to themselves. They are said to be considered very personal possessions. These are exact miniatures of the large masks and were often used to accompany the larger ones in medicine ceremonies. Later they were worn by the person who had been healed as a symbol of recovery. They were also worn as badges of office. Others were simply children's toys.

Many masks and other precious Iroquois family possessions were scooped up and carried home by soldiers who swept through Indian villages in 1779 during the Sullivan-Clinton campaign in New York State. The first masks ever to be put on exhibit in museums, some of them over two hundred years old then, were from that raid.

Today, masks are scarce, controversial, and very expensive. If you happen to own or acquire a very old mask such as a crooked-mouth or perhaps a whistler or corn-husk mask once used with a turtle rattle in a ceremony, you have three choices. One, the Iroquois Indians hope that you might find it in your heart to return it to them so that it can be properly cared for and used according to tradition. Masks are still very sacred to the Iroquois people. Two, you may choose to believe that it should be hung out of sight for fear that strangers who look upon it might become possessed with the power of the mask if they mimic it. Third, you can hang it in open sight and enjoy it as a symbol of man's inner conscience.

Every old mask brings with it a responsibility that no new household can deny!

4

FASHIONS IN DRESS

AN Indian acquaintance, who traveled abroad on a lecture tour last year, was greatly amused to be asked, "Where do you stop and change out of your Indian costume when you go into the cities?" Similar misconceptions regarding Indian dress exist. Too frequently, Indians are visualized in blankets, loin cloths, and moccasins.

In reality, it has been almost two hundred years since Indians of the Northeast made the transition to everyday clothing styles like those of their white neighbors. When they first saw European fashions, the Indians styled their buckskins in the same way. They tended to favor French clothing styles and embroidery motifs. Men wore long hunting coats and leather leggings that very much resembled French military outfits. Women wore coatlike buckskin wraparounds below the knees and leggings in cold weather. All were decorated with porcupine quills; some had brass buttons obtained in trade, and the leather was fringed to allow rain to run off.

By 1760, velvet, silk, broadcloth, and glass beads were commonly used by women in sewing their clothes with needles and thread. They continued to conform to clothing styles of the period and were influenced by lady missionaries (teachers) who taught them to make and embroider clothes. Men still favored buckskin outfits, but the middle 1800s found their everyday clothing to be a pair of dark trousers with a tuniclike, loose-fitting white shirt. An ornately beaded vest was added for more formal occasions. Men also liked wide-brimmed felt hats with a band of decorative silver and a single turkey feather. Women wore long skirts with an overdress of turkey cloth. Embroidery designs in beads and ribbon applique were added. They usually wore many silver brooches and pins on their dresses to indicate prestige. When dressing up, a woman carried a beautiful beaded purse, wore rings, earrings, silver hair ornaments, or perhaps very old bone hair combs. A favorite hat style was a beaded Scotch Glengarry bonnet. Both men and women wore moccasins.

At the end of the 1800s, Indians of the Northeast dressed in the same fashions as whites. Buckskins, beaded vests, ornately decorated dresses, and tribal headpieces were stored away. Authentic native dress

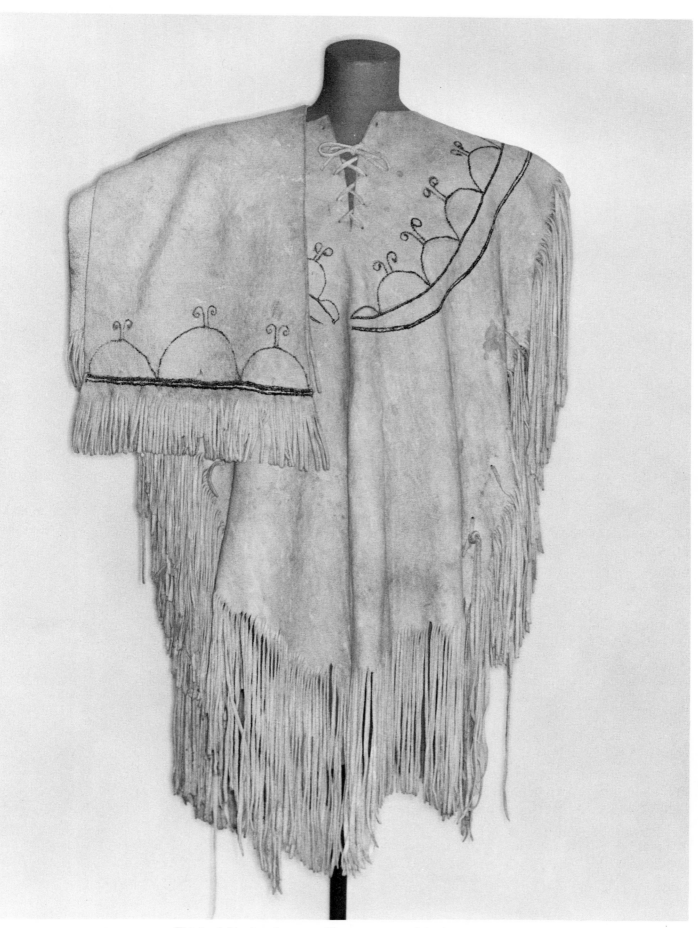

This buckskin dress is a very old museum piece. It had the symbolic sky dome resting on parallel lines representing earth. The tree symbols on top of each sky dome indicate the tree standing alone on the center of the earth; the outward curve of the tree branches symbolizes on-going life. COURTESY OF THE BUFFALO MUSEUM OF SCIENCE.

A man's one hundred-year-old buckskin outfit that is still used at ceremonies just as it was long ago. Today modern Indians make buckskin outfits for themselves.

became a thing of the past except for use in ceremonies and festivals. It has been over a hundred years since some of those authentic costumes were made. Indians of the 1860s couldn't have guessed that their clothing might eventually turn up in attic trunks or treasured collections of historical societies. Why would they be in such places? The answer lies in the practice of adoptions into Indian tribes, which became very popular during the late 1920s and early 1930s. The traditional laws of old for adoptions were often bypassed. Politicians, union leaders, and history buffs were adopted in appreciation for the help many of them gave to poverty-stricken reservations. As part of the ceremony, adoptees were presented with costume apparel as gifts. Often, very old family moccasins,

a vest, or a headpiece were given by the Indian family. Privileged adoptees also paid women on reservations to make them complete ceremonial outfits. Some of these had beautiful moosehair embroidery done by artisans who retained the craft from past generations. Many such outfits are in small-town historical society museums with a photograph of the white adoptee and his blood brothers in full ceremonial costumes.

Some of the people photographed in the late 1920s and early 1930s appear in Hollywood-type Indian garb fashioned after the film characters made of Geronimo, Chochise, and Sitting Bull. Of course, Woodland Indians of the Northeast knew that war bonnets and geometric designs in beadwork were not a part of their long-lost culture; but times and tastes of whites dic-

In contrast to the old Indian buckskins, this ceremonial outfit was made on a reservation for a favored adoptee. The costume was made of velvet, edged with silk, and embroidered with tiny white seed beads. The sleeveless vest, worn over a white tunic, has German silver brooches that were designed and made for him by an Indian silversmith. The ornate sashes have tassels of yarn.
COURTESY OF THE NEUMANN COLLECTION.

This velvet cap, part of the adoptee's ceremonial outfit, has a hand-hammered silver band around the bottom and a single eagle feather on a pivot that rotated as the wearer danced. COURTESY OF THE NEUMANN COLLECTION.

Some of the best photographs done of Indians in contemporary times were those portraits taken at the Pan American Exposition in Buffalo, New York, in 1901. This Seneca Chief was dressed in his buckskin outfit that was embroidered in true Woodland Indian designs. COURTESY OF THE BUFFALO & ERIE COUNTY HISTORICAL SOCIETY.

This girl's attire, photographed against a suitable backdrop, reflects the blending of Victorian fashions (about 1901) with Woodland Indian handcrafts. Note the accessories: Indian-silver brooches, layers of Indian beads, a beaded over-the-shoulder sash, and beautifully embroidered floral cuffs and skirt edges. Leggings were always worn under Iroquois women's skirts. COURTESY OF THE BUFFALO & ERIE COUNTY HISTORICAL SOCIETY.

Photographs of Indian children in ceremonial costumes were seldom done. This beautiful study of an Iroquoian boy on the left and a visiting Plains Indian girl on the right show details and finery lavished on children's clothing. COURTESY OF THE BUFFALO & ERIE COUNTY HISTORICAL SOCIETY.

In 1901, Chief Red Cloud wore those things of which he was most proud or that pleased his tastes. Among these were a bear-claw necklace, a watch on a chain, Indian silver brooches dating back many generations, and medals and badges of white men's fraternal organizations. The expression on his face, the elaborate headpiece, and the chief's cane on which his hand rests, tell the story of cultures blended. COURTESY OF THE BUFFALO & ERIE COUNTY HISTORICAL SOCIETY.

This young woman, photographed in 1889, wore a favored Scotch glengarry-styled hat, silver brooches, and arm bracelets. The white seed-beaded borders on her tunic, skirt, and leggings were decorative touches usually added by Seneca Indians. Doubtlessly, the gun and hatchet were props added by the photographer, for the girl would have been long removed from the use of either of those.
COURTESY OF THE BUFFALO & ERIE COUNTY HISTORICAL SOCIETY.

tated. Clothes made for commercial reasons and those made for personal use were often entirely different in workmanship and aesthetic quality. War bonnets, shields, geometric-designed armbands, and moccasins, along with other Hollywood versions of wearing apparel, were copied from Western motifs. They came after 1900 and fall in the category of valuable and interesting collectibles that reflect a transition in styles, but not the true Northeastern Woodland Indian designs.

The Pan American Exposition held in Buffalo in 1901 triggered this transition to Western motifs. An immense Indian camp ground was established for over three hundred Western Indians who were there in full dress clothes —feathers, shields, ornate beadwork, and flamboyant fashions. The Eastern Indians were

At an outing in the 1920s, Indian women wore combinations in styles. Their outfits reflected personal tastes and the amount of time and effort they wanted to put into them. The three women in the front left and one in the front right were in full Indian costume. The others, dressed in calico overdresses, long skirts with leggings under them, and moccasins were a more usual sight for that period of time. Various nondescript kinds of feathered head creations were worn. COURTESY OF THE BUFFALO & ERIE COUNTY HISTORICAL SOCIETY.

*Tiny moccasins made for Woodland children date about 1850. The
ones on the left are of buckskin; those on the right of corn husks.*
COURTESY OF THE BUFFALO & ERIE COUNTY HISTORICAL SOCIETY.

truly impressed. There was a great deal of trading of headpieces, moccasins, vests, and beaded items.

Your great-grandfather could easily have been given a pair of very old Western Sioux moccasins as a result of his friendship with the people on an Eastern reservation. No fraud was intended! It's just that Indians very often kept their own things and gave away items that had been traded from other tribes. Museum storage collections are filled with donations taken in (accessioned) as, "believed to be," "donor assumes that," "possible Seneca but probably Delaware," because of the continual transferal from one Indian culture area to another. It's too bad that our grandfathers didn't make specific notes, and even more imperative that present owners try to trace where their families acquired apparel items and write it down for future reference.

Moccasins were always sought by outsiders. Those made in the Northeast are distinctive because they were made of leather, soft soled, and had no bottom seam. They were beaded in the same floral designs as clothes. Often, a pair of moccasins matched the designs on a particular dress or vest. A beaded vest and a matching pair of moccasins are very valuable

Each Northeastern Indian group had favorite hat styles. This one, made of turkey feathers with a single rotating eagle feather on top, is typical of the Tuscarora Nation. There was a day when collectors could obtain hats distinctive of the various Indian Nations; but today, any antique headpiece is considered a real find.

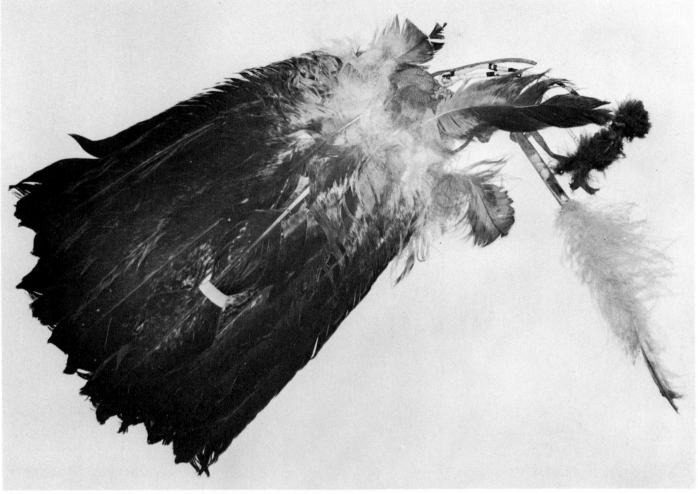

Often, a great deal of meaning is read into Indian items that were just an individual's personal design. This is an old eagle-feather fan. COURTESY OF THE NEUMANN COLLECTION.

items. Headdresses, in authentic Woodland styles, are also prized possessions.

Indian sashes, currently popular due to revived interest in macrame and finger weaving, are excellent examples of skilled craftsmanship. Woven in either a loose or a very tight weave, from possibly as many as a hundred strands of wool, each sash usually combined the Indians' favorite colors —blue, red, black, green, and white. Beaded interweaving on sashes was strictly an Indian innovation. The white beads woven on a special thread in zigzag, diamond, and hexagonal designs, seemed to suggest lightning or arrowheads.

Like moccasins, sashes are thought of as typical Indian items and therefore most desirable to collect. Their popularity explains why many copies of old sashes were machine produced (not by Indians) for sale during the Reservation period. Signs advertising "Indian goods" did not specify that they were Indian made.

Proper storage is essential for preserving these old and fragile items of clothing. A collector may not have the ideal situation but can certainly do better than the damp cellar or dry attic. Clothing should not be packed with plastic dry cleaning bags but rather with tissue paper such as discarded dress patterns. Moccasins, hats, and bonnets likewise should not be stuffed with plastic or newspapers but with tissue. Leather goods sometimes may be stiff and brittle from years of improper care. Today's leather craftsmen, some of whom are Indians specializing in restoring such artifacts, can advise on treating these things.

The important thing is to identify as best as possible, restore, box properly, and select a cool, dry place to store these valuable acquisitions that won't ever come this way again.

5

CORN-HUSK DOLLS

ONE of the most interesting ways to observe the changes in Northeastern Indian clothing tastes is to examine dressed dolls. These dolls, made by mothers and grandmothers for their little girls, were lovingly clothed in cottons and calicoes and daintily beaded with designs similar to those of the grownups' clothes.

Corn-husk dolls are most commonly associated with Indians from the Northeastern part of the United States. Originating with the Iroquois, this craft has undergone many periods of change due to white man's influence. They also made leather dolls and ones with apple faces. This Iroquois craft was also absorbed by other Indian nations.

Originally the dolls were six to twelve inches tall, some with corncob centers, and fully wrapped with husks. They were dressed in husk clothing, skins, or cloth. They had corn-silk hair and no facial features because the Iroquois believed that a doll's facial expression could be seen through a child's own imagination. Today, we pay a lot of money for such play value to be engineered into our children's toys—but two

hundred years ago, Indian parents came by such wisdom naturally. Facial features were added to dolls after contact with white man had occurred.

By 1760, corn-husk dolls reflected the fashions of men, women, chiefs, and warriors of each generation. They were authentically outfitted and had miniature accessories such as beaded cradle boards, bows and arrows, or dance rattles. Miniature corn-husk dolls were also made for play as well as for good luck charms.

There are some outstanding private collections of corn-husk dolls that date from the Reservation period when tourist trade flourished and husk-dolls were popular and selections available. Some of these are proudly preserved in glass domes as they now rank in value with bisque and china dolls from the same period of time. The age of these dolls is evident by the condition of the husks and kind of costume materials and the designs that were used.

Although pre-1900 corn-husk dolls are rare and expensive, once in a while one turns up in a household sale or at an out-of-the- way flea market. After 1900,

A pair of Iroquoian dolls made with leather bodies in about 1800.
These dolls, in very fragile condition, show the style of clothing and
materials used in that period. COURTESY OF THE SMITHSONIAN
INSTITUTION.

dolls made for sale were embellished with features and feathers that made them appealing to white tastes. Other Indian nations that made dolls included Six Nations in Canada, whose distinctive line became very popular. Indian doll collections offer a fascinating opportunity for display and study.

These dolls were made recently by an eighty-six-year-old clan mother. They are classic examples of Iroquoian doll crafts. The dolls stand twelve inches tall and are dressed in husks. The flower designs in the circle medallions are symbolic beadwork from this part of the country. The circle symbolizes a tree and the beads hanging down, its roots. The flower in the medallion has six points, signifying the six Iroquois nations. The headdresses are Mohawk in design.

Aside from being Indian-crafted in the early 1900s, this pair of dolls does not exemplify any pure design or costuming. The added faces and feathers were perhaps intended to make them more appealing for sales purposes off the reservation. COURTESY OF THE POP WARNER COLLECTION.

An unmarried-girl doll wears clothing of the late Reservation period when it was made, about 1915. Her outfit consists of a cotton overblouse in a favorite flowered pattern. A felt skirt opens on the side and the apron has symbolic beadwork and ribbon applique.

This doll, designed and dressed in the style known as the Iroquoian Handsome Lake Religion era, represents the early 1800s. The long overdress was made of calico in a mother hubbard pattern with skirt underneath and leggings. Tiny beaded moccasins are on her feet. All clothing is removable because the doll was made for children's play. Two braids indicate that the doll is unmarried; and the headband, done in Western bead designs, shows the later influences of Western Indian motifs used when the doll was made in about 1900.

The bobbed hair style on this male doll dates it in about 1925. The white shirt, cloth leggings, and apron-type loin cloth were typical Iroquoian dress clothes at that time. The belt and beaded sash that goes over the shoulder were also typical. Beadwork on the apron has points indicating the number of clans (families) in his nation. Leggings are split up the side for easy removal by a child.

A pair of dolls made in about 1900 on an Iroquois reservation.
Woman and man are exact replicas of styles worn then. COURTESY
OF THE POP WARNER COLLECTION.

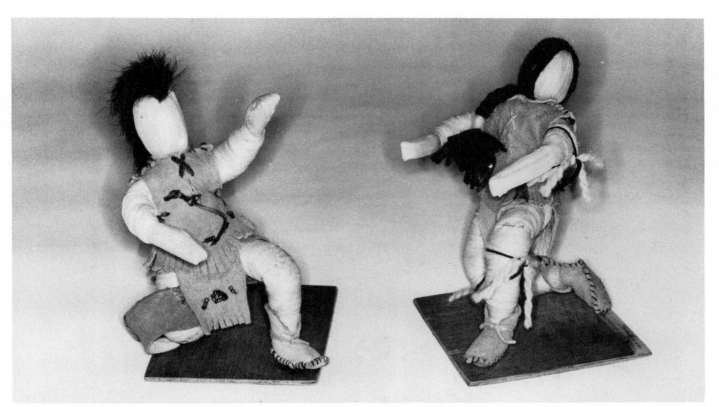

Although of recent vintage, these dolls are exact replicas of Canadian dolls made in characteristic poses beginning in 1900. The body, formed and shaped underneath, is then wrapped with corn husks. Each Indian nation had its own way of stylizing dolls. The man's hair style is that of a Mohawk Indian from the Iroquois nation; the woman's single braid indicates that she is married.

6

SILVER

"I doubt that the average person would recognize a piece of very old Indian silver if he saw it," commented an anthropologist. Likewise, the intrepid Iroquois brave wouldn't have believed that his heirloom silver badge of nationality was actually an upside-down version of the Masonic emblem! Scots introduced the Northeastern Indians to silver long before 1700; but it took historians decades to puzzle out the Masonic emblem that Indians had copied from the Scots as well as other designs in the fascinating 165 years of Indian trade silver and silversmithing in the Northeast.

Silver is one of the few Indian artifacts from which a clear line of history can be traced. Much of it was hallmarked, dated, or engraved with the year of presentation. Early trade and government silver from France and England, peace medals, and fur traders' silver were all made specifically for Indians and are important links to their culture in Northeastern America. However, there are some mysteries that remain unsolved concerning the whereabouts of such silver.

Trade silver refers to those trinkets which early traders showered upon Indians in an effort to win furs and favors. They began trading their own silver buttons, brooches (the Masonic being one of them), belt buckles, rings, and coins. Later the demand resulted in the commercial manufacture and importing of silver ornaments. Indians quickly became knowledgeable about silver —its weight, details of designs, and relative values. The silversmiths who filled orders for these pieces were well known and well paid. Thousands of pieces of thin, highly polished brooches, crosses, gorgets, armbands, rings, and chest ornaments made by Montreal and Quebec silversmiths flowed into this section of America from 1775 to 1825. The Hudson Bay company sent to England for most of its trade silver. In Philadelphia and Pittsburgh, silversmiths produced quantities of armbands, necklaces, medals, and rings to be given to Indians for their alliances and furs. Governments also heaped silver upon the Indians.

Before the American Revolutionary War, lords and ladies in England conversed socially at banquets about

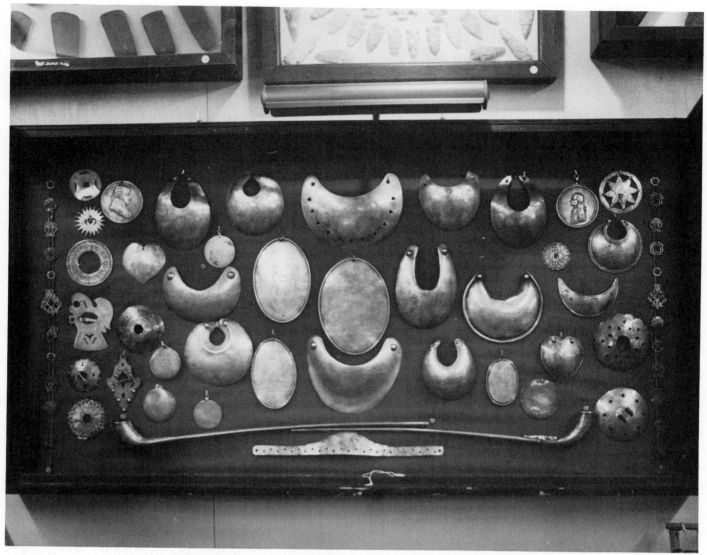

These silver adornments worn by Northeastern Indians during nearly 125 years of silversmithing show large crescent pieces (gorgets) dating before the American revolution; post-Revolutionary War Presidential Peace medals (ovals); and large round brooches and chiefs' emblems used during the fur trade. The vertical ribbons of smaller brooches (extreme left and right) represent some of the Indian made silver pieces produced between 1800 and 1850. Silver pipes and headband at bottom are very rare chief's possession.

decisions being made around council fires in the far away troublesome Colonies of America. At the same time, they complained because fine silver was scarce. Good epergnes were unobtainable and there were few decent pieces of flatware. The hallmarks of England's finest silversmiths continued to be stamped on gifts for chiefs and warriors in Northeastern America. Among them were the initials of Peter Arno, Luke Kendal, Hester Bateman, and George Heming —all of London. Taxes were out of sight, and English gentry hoped that the rebellion would be put down quickly so that their silver needs and tastes might be met again.

This collection of trade-silver brooches and pendants dates between 1780 and 1820. The two center pieces in the top row are variations of the council-fire brooch that was very popular and designed in many motifs. Third brooch down on the left side is the basic compass and arc motif of the traditional Masonic emblem adapted by Northeastern Indians. Star pendant in the center was popular in trade. Bottom row has tiny animal effigy charms as well as a Hudson Bay silver beaver. The pair of brooches on either side of the beaver were symbols of the warrior and have a tomahawk on one end and war club on the other.

Diaries of fur traders and government agents described some Indian families as having bushels of brooches. One Indian might wear as many as three hundred brooches on his everyday clothing. Precious silver had become the status by which he gained prestige. The Indian became even more discerning and demanding as the Revolutionary War drew near and the French, English, and Colonists all tried to influence him.

Gorgets were very popular chest ornaments favored by men. They were crescent-shaped like half moons (probably copied from earlier British officers' gorgets) and are prominently featured in portraits of Northeastern Indian chiefs. The British had an impressive ceremony in which they commissioned Indian leaders as "gorget captains," presenting them with silver gorgets and armbands engraved with royal arms. Brooches, ear ornaments, hairplates, hair bobs, and hair pipes were worn by men and women. Silver crowns, headbands, and hatbands for men were made of sheet silver and often decorated by engraving and pierced work.

Many designs of crosses were also being given to Indians by missionaries during this same period. They varied from an inch to twelve inches in length. Some were elaborately engraved with scrolls and were given to Indians in hopes of persuading them to Christianity. However, the Indians regarded these crosses as ornaments, not religious symbols.

Quakers also offered silver ornaments to induce Indian passive coexistence. It's obvious, therefore, that there was a lot of silver being distributed before the Revolutionary War. It was coming not only from England and France, but also the silversmiths in Philadelphia, Pittsburgh, Montreal, and Quebec. After the war, silver was no longer imported from

French crosses, about 1700, show intricate engraving and varieties of size. Each one was an individual piece of silversmithing and design.

[63]

Two-bar Jesuit cross with proof mark A and a crown at the top. It is not known if the mark was that of a Quebec silversmith or a Paris dating. COURTESY OF IROQRAFTS LTD., OHSWEKEN, ONTARIO.

England in quantity and the United States government instituted the practice of issuing so-called Peace Medals. These were presented to Indians as gifts when their delegates visited the capital, when federal representatives visited Indian country, or at treaty signings and conferences. Each issue had the incumbent United States President's portrait on one side. Peace Medals were issued until 1889.

Silversmiths in the Eastern United States and Canada continued to fill orders for fur-trade silver

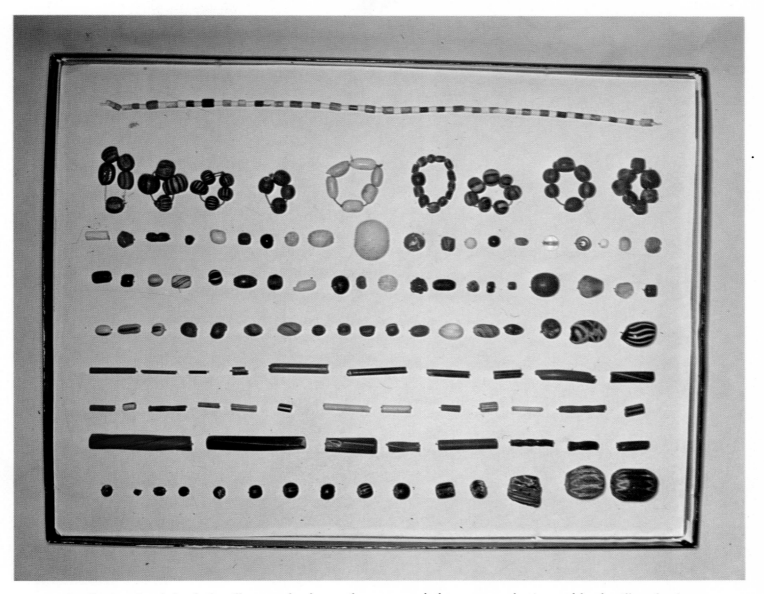

A collection of trade beads that illustrates the changes from some early large ones to the tiny seed beads still used today.

Five examples of purses exquisitely beaded in the old traditions. Beadwork was done in at least four colors representing those in nature, sun, moon, water, and earth. Circa 1860.

A very old pair of Woodland Indian moccasins (left) and a pair made more recently (right) demonstrate beading differences.

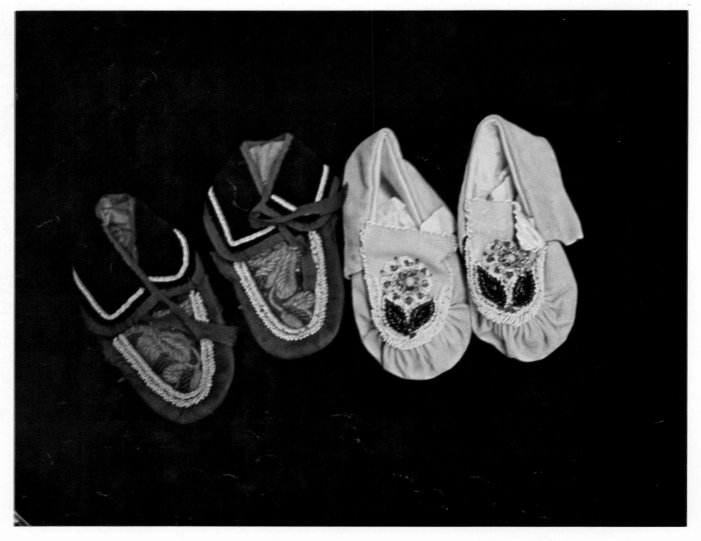

*Joseph Richardson struck the Friendly Association Medals of 1757
in Philadelphia. This front side of the medal shows a bust of George
II with his title.* COURTESY OF THE HISTORICAL SOCIETY OF
PENNSYLVANIA.

Reverse side of the Friendly Association for Preserving Peace with the Indians Medal shows a Quaker seated beneath a tree handing a peace pipe to an Indian by a fire. The sun shines upon their friendship. COURTESY OF THE HISTORICAL SOCIETY OF PENNSYLVANIA.

during the post-Revolutionary War period. The Hudson Bay beaver charm was the most common medium of exchange for pelts. Indians used these silver charms like money. One otter skin earned two charms; two white fox one charm; ten squirrels one charm; and four martens one charm. A charm, in turn, could be traded for any *one* of the following items offered at the fur company trading post: one brass kettle, two ivory combs, eight knives, four spoons, one shirt, two pounds of brown sugar, one pound of Brazil tobacco, or half a pound of thread. Six of the silver beaver charms purchased a blanket and twelve purchased a gun.

Fur-trade silver continued to be in circulation in this part of the country until about 1825. By then, there were skilled silversmiths in most Iroquois villages who worked with German silver and beaten coins to fill an off-reservation market for silver jewelry of Indian

Two early Peace Medals. The George Washington Medal, first issued in 1791, and Thomas Jefferson Medal, 1801, which was struck in three sizes. Notice the details in engravings and differences in the scenes from one year to the next in the Washington issues.

designs. The early Indian-made jewelry was copied from the Montreal silversmiths' designs; eventually, however, Indians developed their own patterns and created unique pieces that sold in jewelry stores in the cities near reservations.

What has become of all this silver? Of the many thousands of pieces of trade silver and Indian silver produced over a hundred-year period, only some is in museums. As for the rest of it, educated guesses are that much of the early silver was turned in by the Indians as each government of a foreign country offered exchange for their issues. The English offered irresistible amounts of their silver for French ornaments already in Indian ownership, and the American government exchanged English silver for United States pieces. This practice of exchanging medals seems to have been very common and systematic as various governments tried to influence Indians. However, no exact records were kept. There are other explanations that help to account for the disappearance of quantities

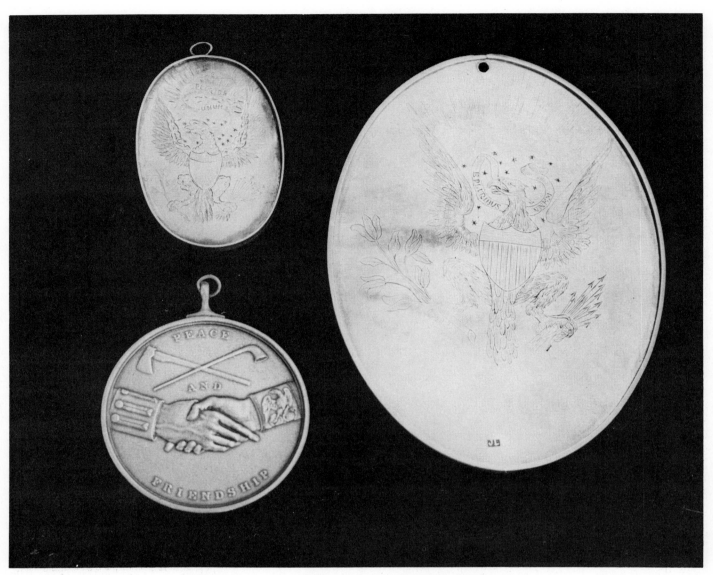

*The reverse sides of the Washington and Jefferson medals showing
changes in the eagle engravings. The hallmark JL on the larger one
probably was that of Joseph Loring of Boston.*

of silver. It is known that much of the silver was buried
with Indians; and that more of it was melted down,
as were the tableware and coins, for raw materials
when Indians began their own silversmithing. More of
it is probably still in private ownership while a great
deal was given and bartered away as Northeastern
Indians were pushed Westward. Some pieces have
turned up mixed with Western Indian silver collections. A lot of it has not as yet surfaced or been recognized as Indian silver from this section of the country.

By knowing the shapes and sizes of silver and some
of the prominent silversmiths' initials, one might
happen across a piece of this unique Northeastern
Indian silver, scarce as it is.

The Treaty of Greenville Medal was issued in 1795 and is the same on both sides. It shows the American eagle with escutcheon on the breast. In his dexter talon is an olive branch; his sinister holds a bundle of fifteen arrows representing fifteen states. Above, the E Pluribus Unum breaks through a cloud. COURTESY OF THE HISTORICAL SOCIETY OF PENNSYLVANIA.

Gorgets were always favorite adornments of Indians and were given as symbols of peace and alliance during the pre-Revolutionary war period. This one, made by silversmith Joseph Richardson of Philadelphia, was commissioned by the Friendly Society for Propagating Peace with the Indians by pacific measures. COURTESY OF THE HISTORICAL SOCIETY OF PENNSYLVANIA.

7

TOYS AND GAMES

VERY early Indian toys are rare. They seem to have been swept away in the tides of death, disease, and destruction. It is those broken pieces and bits of little children's toys that surface, every so often, to nudge our consciences of a forgotten heritage more than anything else.

In addition to dolls, there were miniature wooden utensils and household items, tiny purses, pouches, and baskets made for little girls. There also were carved animals, tops, buzzers, and spools. Many collections have items marked "model of" a bowl, bow and arrow, canoe, or snowshoe. These doubtlessly were children's toys, because the Indians lavished great affection and attention on their youngsters. They took pride in fine, handmade playthings.

Games of skill and chance were played at festivals and some religious ceremonies. Competition was regarded with great esteem, and excellence in sports was considered an attribute. Most sports consisted of team activities that were held with visiting nations or other communities. Individuals were not pitted against each other in sports such as wrestling or boxing. Ball, hoop,

target shooting, and foot races were among the favorites.

It is the game of lacrosse that is considered the national game of the Indians of the Northeast. It is still a tradition. In about 1622, French traders first saw Indians playing a game with rackets that resembled their French bishop's hooked staff, the crozier. Consequently, they dubbed the Indians' sport lacrosse ("the crozier"). The game had some interesting features. For example, there was no limit to team sizes —all the men who wanted to play (sometimes hundreds of them) divided into two teams and played on a field of grass in the summer or on ice in the winter. Games, rough and strenuous, could last days before one team succeeded in scoring the winning goal. Every Indian village had a tree stump that was hollowed in the shape of the hooked end of the sticks. A wet carved stick was wedged in the stump that acted like a template as the wood dried into the proper shape.

Sticks, deer bones, cherry stones, peach stones, and carved wooden tallies were all used in playing games of chance. Some were elaborately carved

[71]

This wooden action toy, carved in the Reservation period, still works. The two figures move to pound corn. COURTESY OF THE HOLLAND PURCHASE HISTORICAL SOCIETY, BATAVIA, N. Y.

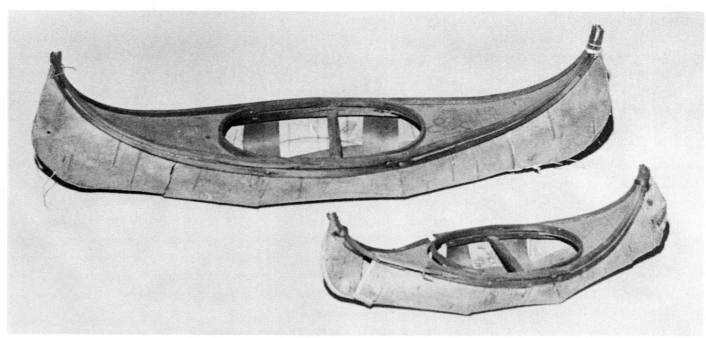

Birchbark canoe models made about 1800 for children's play by Penobscot Indians, Old Town, Maine. COURTESY OF THE SMITHSONIAN INSTITUTION.

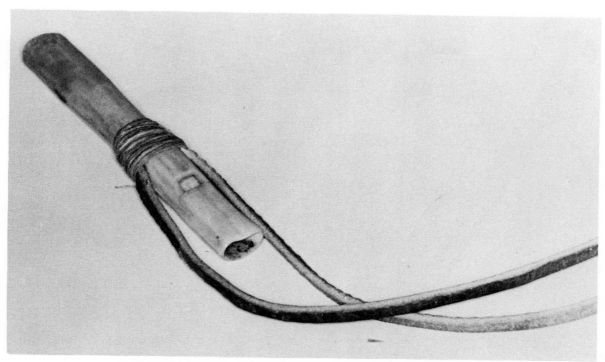

A carved deer-horn whistle that was worn around the neck. It was often used to call children when a family was on an outing in the woods.

because the pursuit of games and sports was more than just a pastime for Indians; it was a philosophy of excellence, fairness, and vigor. These little buttons and counters were carved with dots and delicate designs. Peach stones, used in a dish game, were filed down to look as smooth as a hickory nut. The bowl used in this game was often decorated. These interesting items are often not recognized because they turn up as single items.

Snowsnake, snow boat, and snow shoeing races were sports enjoyed outdoors. Snowsnake has particularly been a favorite sport of Indians from the Northeast. Like lacrosse, its revision in recent years has been added to our heritage of sports in America. The equipment used was simple: slim, polished rods of maple, walnut, or hickory were about an inch thick and from five to nine feet long. A shallow-straight ditch

was laid out in a course in the snow. The object of the game was for the player to throw his rod, making it skim along the course in the ditch. It took tremendous skill. A good thrower could make his snake travel as fast as an arrow and a distance of a thousand to fifteen hundred feet. The thrower whose snake went the farthest in the ditch was the winner.

Target shooting and arrow throwing were also games requiring swiftness and skill. Such exhibitions gave much pleasure to Woodland Indians and were very important in their lives and culture.

Indian families proudly show their antique snow-snakes, snow shoes, and target bows by hanging them in prominent display. The same items were also collected by visitors to reservations who greatly admired the Indians' excellence in sports and who had the pleasure of witnessing such events long ago.

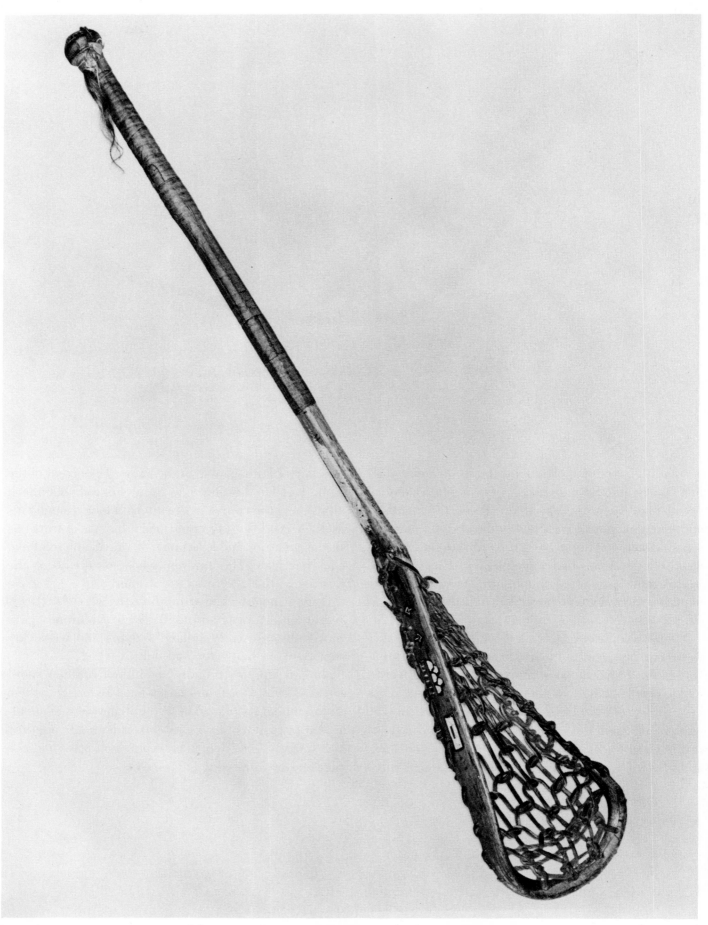

A lacrosse stick from about 1900. Often feathers or ribbons were added to the top of the handle to distract opponents. COURTESY OF
THE NEUMANN COLLECTION.

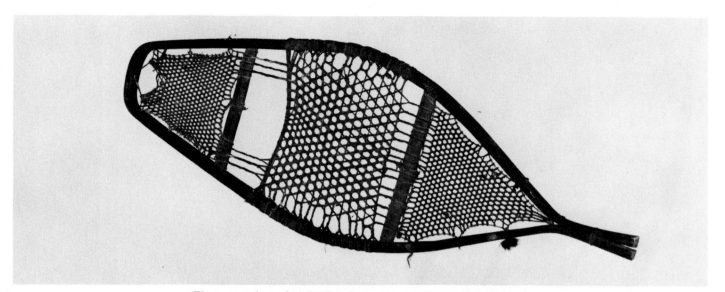

The materials used in this Revolutionary period snowshoe are black ash and wood fiber webbing. In the Northeast, it was impossible to get around in the winter without snowshoes. They were made for men, women, and children and often were collected by outsiders who were fascinated by the Indian's workmanship.

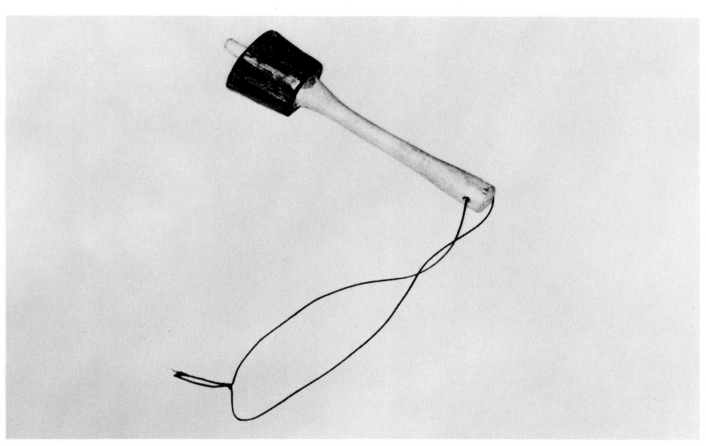

This tiny horn baby rattle filled with dried seeds was usually tied to the cradleboard.

A small boy's carved and shaped bow and arrows with flint points, dating from about 1890. COURTESY OF THE NEUMANN COLLECTION.

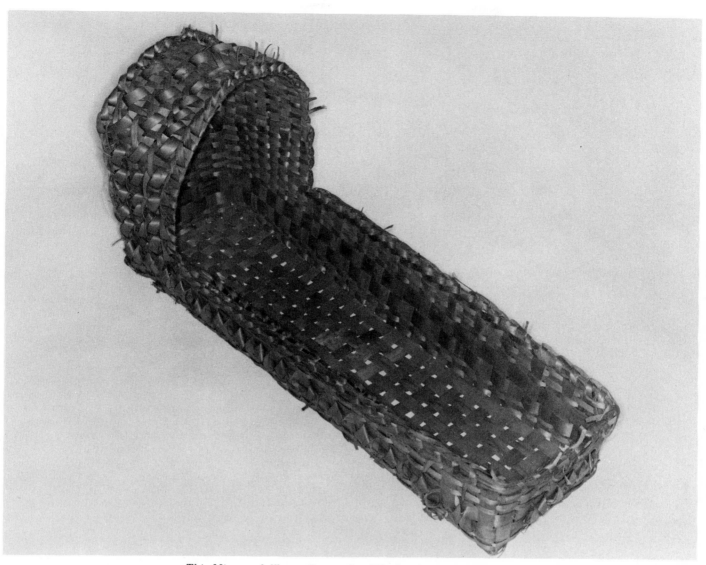

This Micmac doll's cradle, made of black ash, was purchased in New England and dates from about 1880.

8

BASKETS

INDIAN baskets from the Northeast are conspicuous in their simplicity. Unlike the intricate weaving done in the West and Southwest, Northeastern Indians used a basic over and under weave of flat fibers or splints. Constructed primarily for utilitarian purposes the baskets were made of elm bark, corn husks, flags, sweet grass, black ash, and hickory. Except for slight differences in rims and bottoms, all Northeastern Indian baskets are similar in looks.

It sounds overly simple to state that baskets were designed by women who wanted to put things away! If you stop to realize that Indians didn't originally have bureaus, cabinets, and hutches in which to keep possessions, early basket styles make sense. Therefore, Indian basketry included hampers —some tall, others rectangular —in which to store clothes; baskets for gathering all kinds of garden produce —big, deep corn-washing baskets; shallow cornmeal sifting baskets; back packs; fish baskets; and even tiny miniatures made for little girls' play. The same over and under weaving was also used to make items such as bags, nets, mats, moccasins, cages, and bedding.

Because of the perishable characteristics of plant fibers used in basketry, examples of these truly old utilitarian baskets of the Northeast are generally limited to museum collections.

As times changed, so did the basket designs. The craft had to meet the demand of a growing market off the reservations. Indian baskets created pleasant mental images of women harvesting corn, beans, and squash in sunny fields, and of grandmothers contentedly weaving sweet grass into dainty containers. From 1875 on through the depression years, many baskets were made for sale on city streets and at country fairs throughout the Northeast. While the workmanship was authentic Indian basketry, the items reflected the homes and wares of outsiders. Comb baskets, purses, serving baskets for breads and maple sugar, berry baskets, card trays, cake carriers, sewing baskets, tiny thread and needle cases, picnic hampers, and laundry baskets were popular items. Details such as curls, checkered plaiting, and border decorations were added to the basic art for enhancement.

[78]

These styles, typical of the kinds of utilitarian baskets made by Indians in the Northeast and dating from about 1850, were done in a simple weave of black-ash-saplings. The large one in the rear was used for harvesting and storing fruits and vegetables; the one in the lower left was for washing fruits and vegetables; and the one in the right was a household basket. COURTESY OF THE NEUMANN COLLECTION.

At the top left is a market basket made of plain woven black ash with a carved black-ash handle. Next to it is a decorative basket made to hold a woman's special things, and in the bottom row are some of the more fancy baskets made for sale. At the bottom left is a sweet-grass strawberry basket and next to it a sewing basket of sweet grass with tiny needle and thread inserts. These date about 1900.

The antiquity of these old baskets is evidenced by style, color, and workmanship. Hopefully, one's grandparents or great-great-grandparents stored them with care; but, in many instances, extremes in temperatures in attics or cellars have taken a toll on them. They may be mildewed or brittle; however, it is possible to recondition them. Since the revival of this old craft, some Indians now offer repair work on baskets.

Reconditioning requires some know-how, however, and a few pointers should be kept in mind. Don't try to wash dirt off. Start with a very soft toothbrush and go over fibers gently. The soft brush of a vacuum cleaner can pick up loose dirt as you go along. Work gently but consistently to remove this surface dirt. Some collectors try carbon tetrachloride or a damp cloth on a very inconspicuous part of a basket to test stain removal. Many others won't tempt fate and simply brush off loose dirt and charge the rest to original condition. Airing will take away musty odors. Exposure to slight dampness such as steam from showering might help brittleness, but approach this idea with caution.

Proper storage and display are most important to the

This late 1800 black-ash tote basket was a common household item used for carrying cornbread and other foods. The cover closed to keep foods clean. The durability of black ash is proven by the age of the basket. A wire for hanging to display is shown properly looped about the plaiting.

This Reservation period open-weave sieve basket was a standard item in every Indian household and a popular collector's item for others.

A birchbark basket, typical of Canadian styles, decorated with quills of sweet grass. Made in the Reservation period.

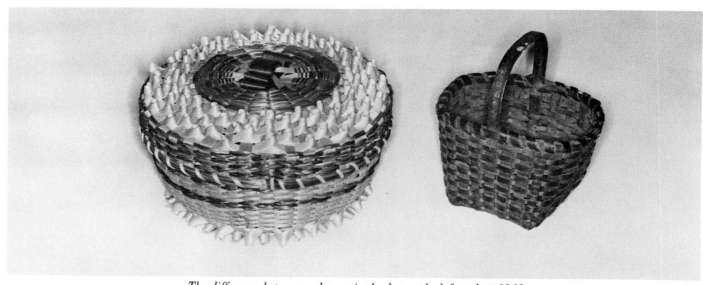

The difference between a decorative basket on the left and an 1860 berry-gathering basket on the right is in materials from which they were made. The decorative basket is made of sweet grass with applied looping and the utilitarian one is of black ash.

This Iroquoian strawberry basket dates approximately at 1900. It is made of sweet grass and has applied decorative looping. This was a favorite of collectors because of the folklore associated with it. It was told that the Iroquois often buried such a favorite basket with their dead because they believed that the path to heaven is bordered by strawberries; they wanted their loved one to be able to gather them on his journey.

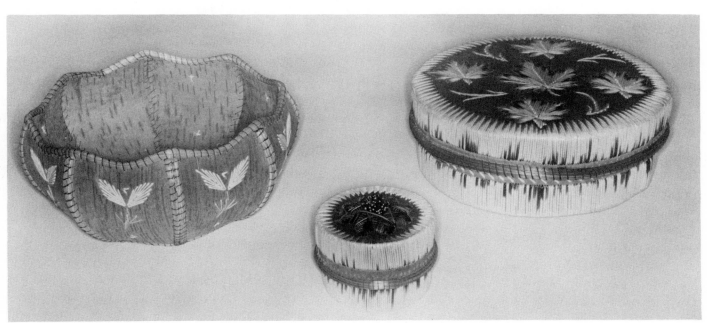

These Canadian birchbark baskets with applied quill designs are contemporary examples of the early Reservation period baskets made for tourist sales there. They reflect the Algonkian influences on basket styles in the Northeast.

Sweet grass was also used for purses and totes. This purse was made about 1900 and is still usable. It has been rinsed in water for cleaning many times over the years. Rolled sweet grass, applied in floral motifs such as this, is sometimes mistaken for the older craft of porcupine quillwork on objects.

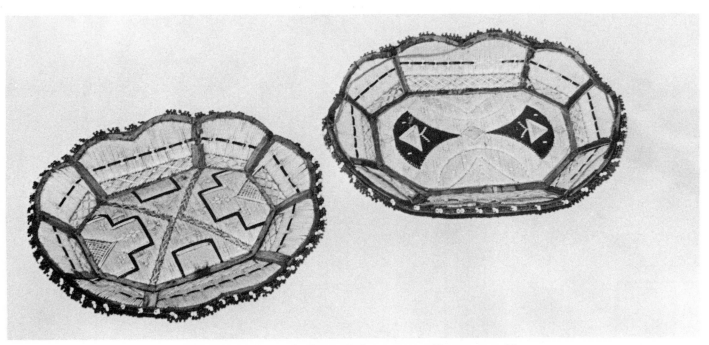

Micmac sweet grass baskets with deep green and brown vegetable-dyed quills used for intricate designs. Made in the Reservation period, circa 1860, for sale in Canada or New England as calling card trays, these were often used as table mats for hot dishes. COURTESY OF THE SMITHSONIAN INSTITUTION.

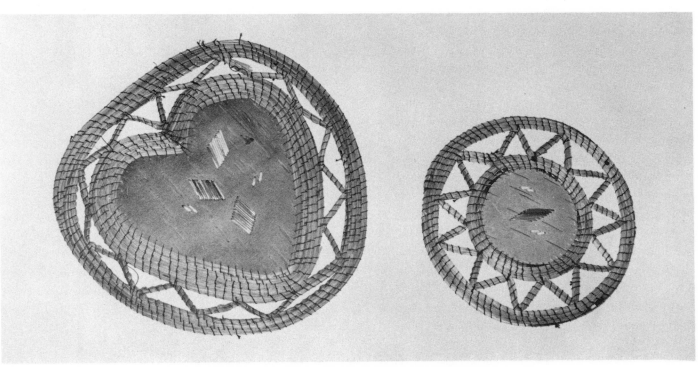

Examples of Canadian birchbark hot-dish mats made for sale.

An Indian Basket Sale
— At The —
BAPTIST CHURCH
Thursday, March 29th

Easter Baskets, made by the Cattaraugus Indians. All sizes and shapes. Filled with Easter Candy, if you wish.

Some very nice Auto Baskets.

Wait for this Sale.   Remember the Date !

ANNOUNCEMENT!

B. R

B

A 1923 want ad illustrates the popularity of Indian baskets in this section of the country. Many people may not realize that their old baskets could be of Indian craftsmanship. PHOTO COURTESY OF THE AURORA HISTORICAL SOCIETY MUSEUM.

long life of these very old Indian baskets. A glass bookcase or cupboard is ideal. Some people have shelves on the walls, and keep a moist sponge on a dish or little foil trays of water in various spots along the shelf to add moisture. One couple, with an exquisite lifetime collection, keeps all baskets in an air-conditioned room. Baskets to be hung on a wall should have a light wire loop added. This is better than punching through the fiber with a nail. Regular dusting and checking for bugs is important. Moth balls in foil containers set inside baskets will discourage mice and pests. Soft tissue, not plastic dry cleaning bags, can be crumpled inside baskets to help retain shapes. Discarded dress patterns are excellent for this purpose.

Baskets —Indian baskets in particular —have always been a popular collector's item. They show up frequently in shops and at shows. Once recognized, they sell for prices ranging from thirty-five to one hundred dollars, depending on condition. Even those very old ones in poor condition are being purchased eagerly.

9

HOUSEHOLD ITEMS

BY 1760, the Indian home was a combination of native goods (both ceremonial and utilitarian) and trade goods. The women raised chickens and pigs, picked fruits from their orchards, harvested corn, beans, squash, berries, and nuts. Men hunted, trapped, ran their tanneries and fish hatcheries, and traded furs for household necessities, hunting goods, and cheap alcohol that was eagerly offered them. Life, for the women, was passive in philosophy but not peaceful. All around them there were skirmishes and raids (in both directions, Indians attacking whites and whites attacking Indians) as the rough and rugged frontiersmen continued pushing on to Indians' lands for hunting, grazing, lumbering and crop planting.

It seems natural to imagine that Northeastern Indians moved directly from stockaded longhouse settlements to reservations. Actually, they had completed a slow transition from living in communal dwellings to occupying private cabins similar to those of their white neighbors. Neighbors, in those days, meant no one closer than ten miles! By 1760, four generations of outsiders from Europe had been born

and reared here. They were entrenched American backwoodsmen and felt nothing in common with the far away homelands of their great-grandparents. For Indians, the old days of longhouses and stockades were gone, and their villages were settlements of log cabins with a central council-meeting house in each village. Trapping and trading at forts or fur company posts or with white traders or neighbors who came to their villages had become their whole economy.

Over the ensuing years, Indian-cabin styles changed just as whites did. First there were rough log and bark cabins; after the Revolution hewn log cabins appeared; and in the early Reservation period, pine cabins prevailed. Small frame houses came in the 1900s.

Inside these homes there were husk or fur rugs on the floors; primitive but sturdy furniture similar to that of the whites; and a fireplace with cooking pots, metal ladles, and serving spoons. They used mattresses of braided husks, fur, or Hudson Bay blankets. There were cradles, cradleboards, bead looms, storage boxes and pouches, toys, and decorative sweetgrass

Traces of the Revolutionary War period are to be found in the original old floor and log foundation of this cabin on the Cattauragus Reservation in western New York. The cabin still conveys the feeling of a typical Indian home in the late 1700s.

This interior view of an Indian cabin makes obvious the fact that the Indians, by 1790, had absorbed into their lives many of the products of whites. The cabin was once opened as a special exhibit.
COURTESY OF THE BUFFALO & ERIE COUNTY HISTORICAL SOCIETY.

baskets. Pouches of tobacco, herbs, and gourds hung from the beams to dry. Their cabins very much resembled those of whites in the same economic class.

Indians excelled at food preservation and preparation, and were very conscious of what we today call ecology and the environment. They added far more food items to white men's diets than they ever copied — corn, beans, squash, hominy, succotash, and maple syrup are just a few. Even today their knowledge of natural foods rates high on the health-foods lists.

It was during and immediately after the Revolutionary War that their homes, orchards, and fields were destroyed and they had to begin anew, clinging in vain to the old ways while new times overwhelmed them. During this period, 1779 to 1800, possessions became a jumble as people were uprooted from one living area to another.

An Indian family's antique treasures may include an eight-hundred-year-old-pot, and a pre-Revolutionary War beaded wall pocket. Also there might be a favorite ironstone bowl indicating that it's not unusual for them to prize valuable and rare antiques of white men's manufacture that were handed down in their own families.

A corn pounder stood next to every cabin for daily use. This one-hundred-year-old pounder was hollowed out of a tree stump. It is 3½ feet high and is still used on the reservation when traditional foods are prepared for festivals or open-house events.

Inside each cabin, there were cradleboards for babies. This one is Senecan, elaborately carved and dates about 1814. Straps and beading are missing. COURTESY OF THE HOLLAND PURCHASE HISTORICAL SOCIETY, BATAVIA, N. Y.

This is one of many sizes in cast-iron cooking pots that were manufactured for trade with Indians. COURTESY OF THE WOODLAND INDIAN CULTURAL CENTRE, BRANTFORD, ONTARIO, CANADA.

Once an everyday ordinary bowl and ladle used in food preparations, this is now a very valuable antique from the Reservation period, dating about 1870.

This perfect twenty-four-inch-wide slippery elm-bark basket was donated for a museum opening in 1894. Such baskets were common in Indian homes in the early 1800s. COURTESY OF THE HOLLAND PURCHASE HISTORICAL SOCIETY, BATAVIA, N. Y.

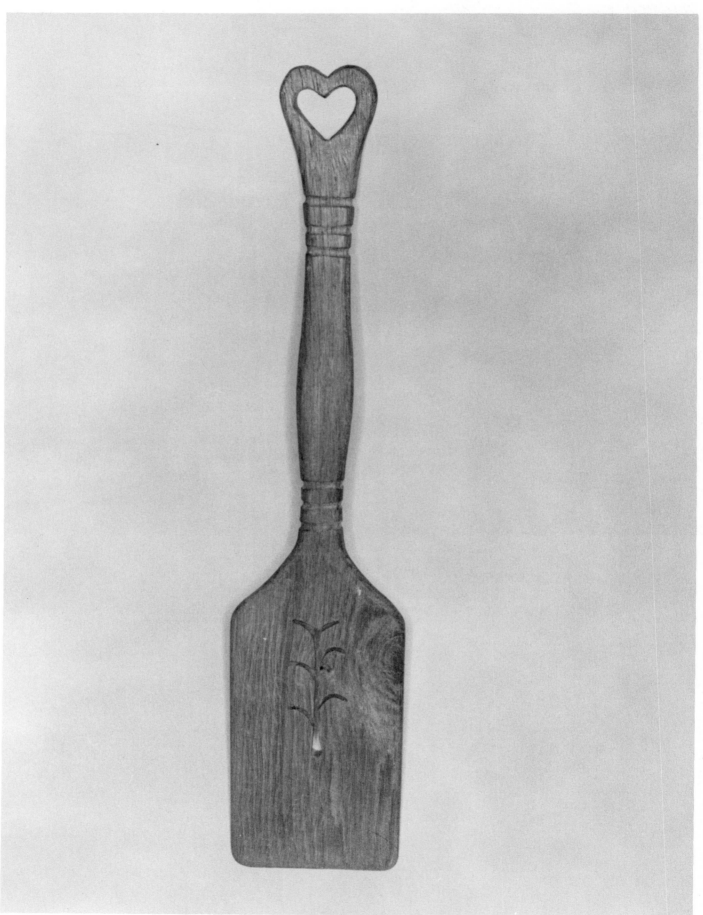

This is a replica of the kind of food paddle carved by Indians of the Northeast. It is used at festivals for stirring foods in huge iron cooking pots.

A corn-husk salt bottle (stopper missing) dating about 1900. It was a common household item for Indians and also was made for sale off the reservations. COURTESY OF THE NEUMANN COLLECTION.

These carved-bone spoons, used for ceremonial food eating, date in the late 1800s. COURTESY OF THE NEUMANN COLLECTION.

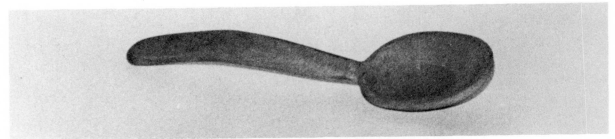

This Mohegan teaspoon, carved from light wood, dates about 1800. COURTESY OF THE SMITHSONIAN INSTITUTION.

These Mohawk wooden spoons date about 1875. Such spoons were often carved for ceremonial use only. By 1875, Northeastern Indians used tableware and dishes similar to their white neighbors. It shouldn't be assumed that they sat cross-legged on the floor eating from bowls of wood. COURTESY OF THE SMITHSONIAN INSTITUTION.

This Iroquoian wraparound skirt with delicate beaded designs dates from the early Reservation period. The half-circles (or domes) symbolize the sky, the parallel lines represent earth, and along with the tree designs, these were favorite border decorations.

The embossed beading on this Iroquoian man's hat is elaborate and exquisitely done.

The Trade Room inside Old Fort Niagara at Youngstown, New York, is atmospheric and authentic in details. The items on display represent goods manufactured for the French, British, and American governments as well as for the Hudson Bay Fur Company. They are typical of the kinds of products offered to Indians at such forts throughout the east. Colonists also shopped at these trade rooms.

There are seldom authentic identifying marks that distinguish a mortar as being Indian made. There are many old pestles and mortars, but a collector would be mistaken to accept and pay for this one as being Iroquoian, made at St. Regis in 1875 (which it was) unless he could have the source verified. COURTESY OF THE SMITHSONIAN INSTITUTION.

This mortar and pestle are authenticated as Mohawk, dating about 1870. These things were used daily in everybody's homes for crushing herbs, spices, salt, corn, and sugar. It is debated whether Indians taught or learned from whites how to make and use them. COURTESY OF THE C. S. HICK COLLECTION, SULLIVAN COUNTY, NEW YORK.

The corn-husk floor mat was really a by-product from the daily use of corn and the piles of husks that accumulated. Recycling of by-products is no new concept to Indians. Their husk, bone, horn, bark fiber, and leather crafts reflect inventiveness at using leftovers.

This common-type carved serving dish was inscribed "St. Regis 1875, R. B. Hough" by the man whose collection of Mohawk items was donated to the Smithsonian. COURTESY OF THE SMITHSONIAN INSTITUTION.

A ceremonial succotash bowl that was owned by a chief of a Connecticut tribe. It dates from the 1700s and has carved bear handles. Animals were often carved on eating utensils. COURTESY OF THE HOLLAND PURCHASE HISTORICAL SOCIETY, BATAVIA, N. Y.

This twenty-two-inch-long carved maple-sugar mold illustrates the Christian influence on some Indians of the Northeast. It was made in about 1899. COURTESY OF THE SMITHSONIAN INSTITUTION.

10

TRADE GOODS

The Great Spirit, when he made the earth, never intended that it should be considered merchandise. His will is that all his creatures should enjoy it equally.

Seneca

FROM the time that the Dutch gave twenty-four dollars worth of beads for Manhattan until the last fur traders moved West over two hundred years later, whole industries came and went in a lop-sided commerce with Indians. This process was called trade.

The simple truth is that in spite of all that happened in those early years of America's history, there was nothing in the Indian's philosophy that made him understand the meaning of lying. Since he truly believed that land was a gift of the Creator and could not be privately possessed, the Indian was amused that white men thought they were buying it from him for a trinket or string of pretty beads. To his way of thinking, it was not his to trade and the mathematics of measurements or scribblings on a document meant nothing. Likewise, at first one pelt for one trinket didn't seem relatively out of proportion. As pelts got

scarce and the Indians' economy depended entirely on trade goods, hunting and trapping became a desperate struggle for Indian groups throughout the Northeast. They were pitted against each other in a situation of survival of the fittest. The Iroquois Nations won — temporarily.

Perhaps his values eventually would have lined up with white men's way of doing business had it not been for alcoholism and conflicting religious teachings that finally completely confused the Indians' thinking. By the middle of the 1800s, he was written off, in white diaries, as drunken, lethargic, and without gumption.

Guns and whiskey were the two most sought after items to be obtained from white agents who came to Indian country or at the forts and fur-company trade posts. There was a steady procession of Indians going to these places with bundles of pelts to trade for guns, liquor, tobacco, groceries, and housewares. Early guns, offered to the Indians in the Northeast by the French and English, were often castoffs that government inspectors had branded as seconds or rejects. These were often far more hazardous to the Indian

Flintlock muskets were traded for pelts. The slope of this stock indicates early 1700s. An important feature in this section of the country was a large trigger guard that enabled the gun to be discharged when the finger was enclosed in a mitten. **COURTESY OF THE OLD FORT NIAGARA ASSOCIATION, YOUNGSTOWN, NEW YORK.**

than to his enemy because of the imperfections that caused them to explode in the user's face. In this country by 1760, the Brown Bess, the Kentucky long and short rifles, and the Ferguson were given in trade. In the middle 1800s, the Hudson Bay Company issued trade guns made in factories in the United States and Europe. Commonly referred to as Fukes, the Northwest gun, or Mackinaws, they appeared only briefly in the East before going on with fur traders to the West. Sometimes these guns had a distinctive dragon orna-

ment or a presentation plaque on them. Trade guns are rare and difficult to document. Of the thousands of guns manufactured in Europe and America, very few survived; some are in private collections. Many of them disintegrated in arsenals because of rust and many more were recalled and melted down when new weapons were manufactured.

Crooked knives for carving, hammers, beads, pouches, yard goods, hardware, threads, needles, and wearing apparel offered at trade stores were common

Powder horns were also popular with the Indians. Even though they made their own, they also liked those of military issue. COURTESY OF THE OLD FORT NIAGARA ASSOCIATION, YOUNGSTOWN, NEW YORK.

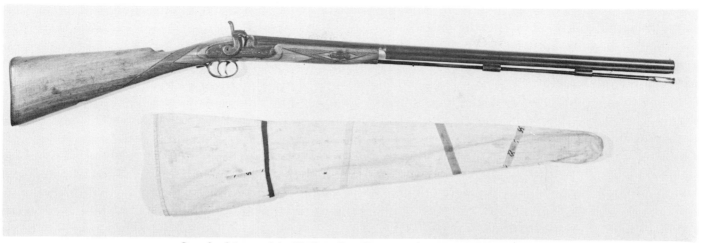

Standard issue of the Hudson Bay Company forty-six-inch barrel trade rifle, dating in the middle 1800s. PHOTOGRAPH COURTESY OF MUSEUM OF THE AMERICAN INDIAN, HEYE FOUNDATION, NEW YORK CITY.

Many sizes and styles of brass kettles were offered in trade. The bottom shelf pictures a yoke and old scale with hooks and weight in the center. COURTESY OF THE OLD FORT NIAGARA ASSOCIATION, YOUNGSTOWN, NEW YORK.

Tobacco was the most important trade item for Indians. Trade rooms were filled with bunches of it hanging from the rafters. A perfect brass kettle, such as the one shown here, would be a rare find today. COURTESY OF THE OLD FORT NIAGARA ASSOCIATION, YOUNGSTOWN, NEW YORK.

items. Axes were also popular trade items. Often mistakenly labeled as tomahawks, they were tools for everyday use. Many of these items that were made for trade had government or military emblems on them. HB identified the Hudson Bay company's items. Sometimes the name of the reservation for which goods were manufactured was stamped on them. Special units had handmade metal plates with a chief's name engraved along with a presentation date.

Trade goods are necessarily a part of Indian antique inheritances just as are the things crafted by their own people.

The candle molds on the top shelf were doubtlessly for Colonists. Jugs of liquor would have been of interest to both Indian and white men. COURTESY OF THE OLD FORT NIAGARA ASSOCIATION, YOUNGSTOWN, NEW YORK.

Trade ax with Indian beads. COURTESY OF THE OLD FORT NIAGARA
ASSOCIATION, YOUNGSTOWN, NEW YORK.

Mortars and pestles in wood and metal were everyday necessities for preparing foods. COURTESY OF THE OLD FORT NIAGARA ASSOCIATION, YOUNGSTOWN, NEW YORK.

Typical trade ax manufactured for many years. COURTESY OF THE
NEUMANN COLLECTION.

*A pocket tobacco tin made of silver was a highly prized trade object.
This one still has old tobacco in it.* COURTESY OF THE NEUMANN
COLLECTION.

11
ARROWHEADS

ARE arrowheads to be considered antiques as well as relics? Yes! Points (usually called arrowheads), like beadwork and baskets, can logically be included in the antique possessions of Indian families. Similarly, boxes full of arrowheads can be found in white men's homes. Many generations of Indians have practiced the art of flint chipping, pecking, grinding, polishing, and carving with bone or modern tools. After white men gained dominance of the land, and Indian men were thereby deprived of their greatest role as hunters and providers, they perhaps took some small comfort in identifying with the ancient craft of making points. An old timer who received his bone flint-chipping tools and an arrowhead collection from the reservation where he was adopted in early 1900 said, "They belonged to my adopted sister's great-great grandfather."

Generally speaking, people call all points arrowheads. The correct term however is *projectile points*. These were made for spears, darts, and arrows as well as for use as blades (similar to our jack knives and penknife blades). The exact uses for many of the points of different length and thicknesses are still only educated guesses.

The thought that one might find an arrowhead in the ground is most intriguing! Every spring, these artifacts continue to rise to the surface as a result of earth moving. No Indian relic collector can resist nosing around newly plowed farm fields, excavation sites where bulldozers have churned up the earth, or along streams as the waters move away layers of earth. It's a chance to find a valuable antique without cost, and each arrowhead turned up brings with it a definite slice of history that can date back thousands of years. "Seeing arrowheads is like spotting four leaf clovers," said a farm woman, "your eye just learns to spot them when spring plowing starts. Some folks could never see a point. Of course, it was much easier when we used a horse and plow because it was slower and the rider sat nearer the ground. People still come out here each spring and walk the fields and river bank looking for arrowheads. And they find them, but not as readily as we did when I was a little girl almost eighty years ago!"

Archaeologists have established the fact that there

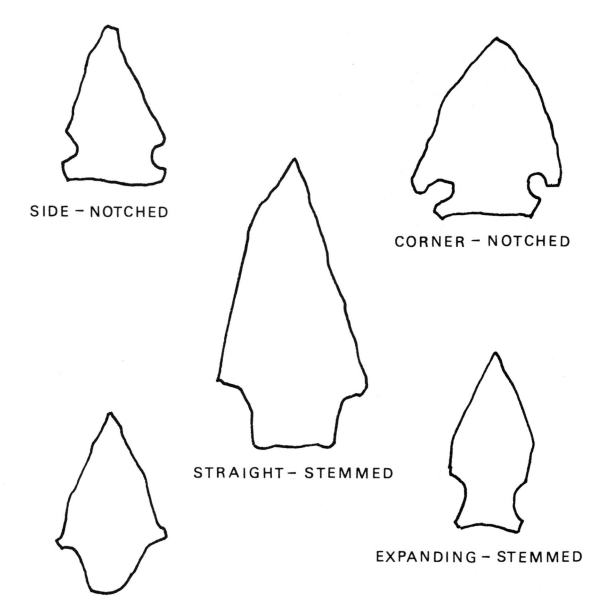

SIDE – NOTCHED

CORNER – NOTCHED

STRAIGHT – STEMMED

CONTRACTING – STEMMED

EXPANDING – STEMMED

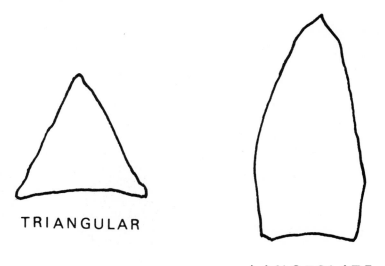

TRIANGULAR

LANCEOLATE

These are point outlines. Anyone with an arrowhead collection can spread them out and identify them according to basic shapes. Points have a five-thousand-year history, so this basic identification is only the beginning in a complex and fascinating study. DRAWING BY RIX JENNINGS.

A prized possession of an adoptee was this set of horn-flaking tools and pounding stone for making arrowheads. Along with the gift came lessons in point chipping. COURTESY OF THE NEUMANN COLLECTION.

These points labeled, "From a farm in Pennsylvania," are an ordinary assortment of common types. Some interesting things can be done with them. COURTESY OF THE POP WARNER COLLECTION.

One of the baskets full of arrowheads accumulated over the years by a farm family. COURTESY OF MRS. BERNICE C. REES.

were definite fashions in point styles. Without knowing it, Indians as far back as twelve thousand years ago may have conformed in point styles. Points from the same depths in the earth throughout a given vast area in the country are similar in shape, length, width, and thickness. A scientific procedure called carbon-14 testing proved them to originate from the same time periods. Since projectile points are indestructible, they tell us more about Indian prehistory than do many other relics. They are a study in themselves and are mentioned in this book only insofar as they pertain to antique collecting.

Let the buyer beware because there is a decided difference between Indian-made arrowheads and Indian arrowheads. Thousands of fakes have been turned out and people unknowingly buy them for three dollars to twelve dollars where they are displayed in dusty, old-looking boxes. Often a dealer has no idea that he is passing on a fake. One honestly commented that, "An arrowhead is an arrowhead, isn't it?" No! Advertisements offering Indian arrowheads do not always claim that their items are either antiques or relics. Although you'd think it's not easy to fake thousands of years of age, a beginner needs coaching in order to differentiate an ancient arrowhead from one that is recently made.

Point collecting as an investment requires study and knowledge. Purchases from a reputable Indian-relic

Here are examples of points sorted and arranged in wall displays.
Top row (middle frame) contains wampum strings. Next to it, is a
collection of other relics from farm sites. As shown, arrowheads can
be used for interesting and imaginative interior decorating ideas.

dealer should be guaranteed in writing as to authenticity. Another qualified source of authentic items would be a private owner who had picked the points from the earth as the following illustrates.

"We figure this farm must have been a hunting party's campsite over the years," said a woman as she poured shoe boxes full of points onto the table. "Every spring we plow them up like this!" Her farm sits on the edge of a stone quarry; it was obviously a convenient place for Indians to gather easily chipped pieces of flint. This particular woman was interested enough to have a nearby university's archaeology department identify, classify, and date her collection.

Basically, there are two systems for identifying points. One is a geographical identification, that is by the name given them from the site where they were first discovered. Examples are the Ashtabula point from Ashtabula, Ohio, and Jack Reef points from a site known as the Jack Reef site, Onondaga, New York. Other geographic locations of rivers, creeks, mounds, and culture areas are numerous.

The other system is identification of points by their shape or outline. This method is probably best for a beginner in order to familiarize himself with the different styles in points.

When buying at flea markets, shows, and auctions, concentrate on points from your own section of the country. Learn to identify the materials and point styles common to your region. Study nearby museum collections. When you've looked carefully at enough of them, you'll become familiarized with point styles and materials natural to the Northeast.

No collector wants to pay for or display an arrowhead that could be less than a month old and produced in five minutes. Do your homework and then enjoy the pleasure of sorting and artistically displaying an authentic point collection. There are societies of point collectors. Contact a local science museum for leads. If you are among the families who own such collections, they will grow in value all the time. You should get them identified.

12
WAMPUM

THE word *wampum* was a broad translation into English of an Algonkian expression for a string of white shell beads. Nothing is more controversial and misunderstood than wampum. The word itself can evoke charges of grave robbing and treaty breaking. Large antique auction houses no longer want to handle it. Some courts have ruled in favor of the Indians demanding the return of sacred wampum belts from museum showcases to Indian council houses. There are strong emotions about treaty belts, condolence and tribal message belts, removed from the graves of chiefs. The ownership of sacred wampum by outsiders is a touchy subject.

Many people are not really familiar with what wampum is or what it looks like. A variety of bone, shell, stone, and wooden beads and ornaments once offered in trade are often incorrectly labeled as wampum. Wampum was made from seashells. A piece of shell was broken off and carved into round or oblong shapes. It was a slow, tedious process when done with bone tools. White wampum was made from the pyrula shell and purple from the purple spot on the quahog clam shell. The tiny tubular beads, less than a quarter of an inch long and an eighth of an inch thick, were strung on threads of deer sinew or bark fibers.

Wampum dates back to the origin of the Iroquois Confederacy and was first used as a way to record messages. It played a major role in the first two hundred years of commerce in the Northeast. As far back as 1600, when the first Dutch traders reached Manhattan, they saw Indians cutting clam shells, perforating them, and making strings. The beads were irregular, slightly angular in shape, and varied in sizes up to an inch long. Because of the labor involved and the sacred significance, wampum was not only scarce but considered precious by the Indians. They showed little appreciation for the gold and silver of new arrivals insofar as trading power went. With steel tools, the Dutch improved and quickened wampum-bead production and launched it into a medium of exchange. They made and offered twenty-three inches of white or twelve inches of the scarcer purple shells for an Indian's beaver skin. Wampum became a convenient substitute for money and one mutually agreeable to all

[117]

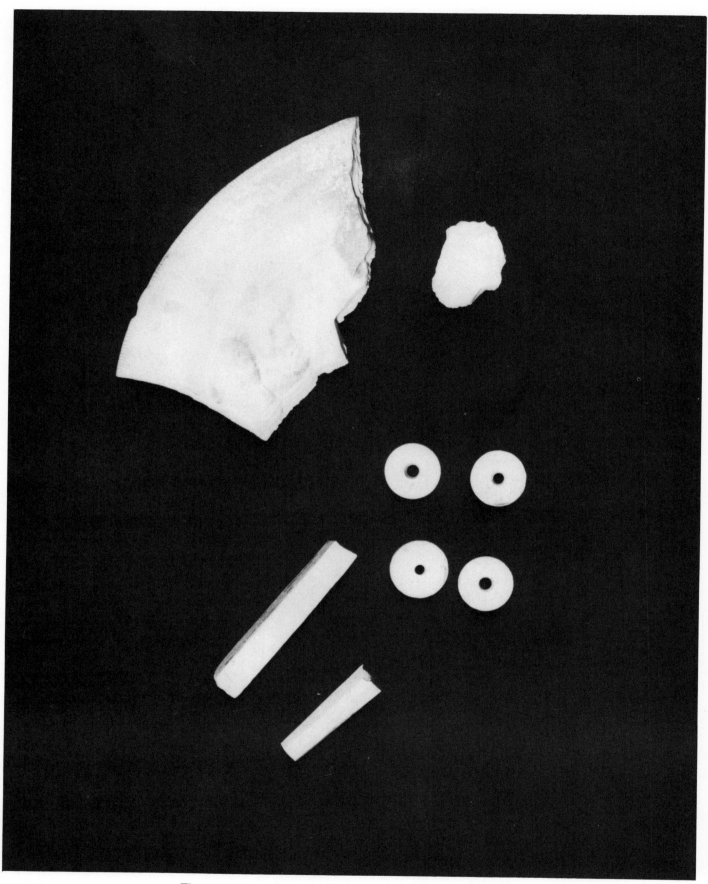

Wampum was made from seashells. A piece of shell was broken off and carved into round or oblong pieces. When originally produced by bone tools, the task was tedious and exacting. Hand-drilled holes in these beads are not uniform and go through in a cone-like angle, indicating that the beads were not commercially produced.

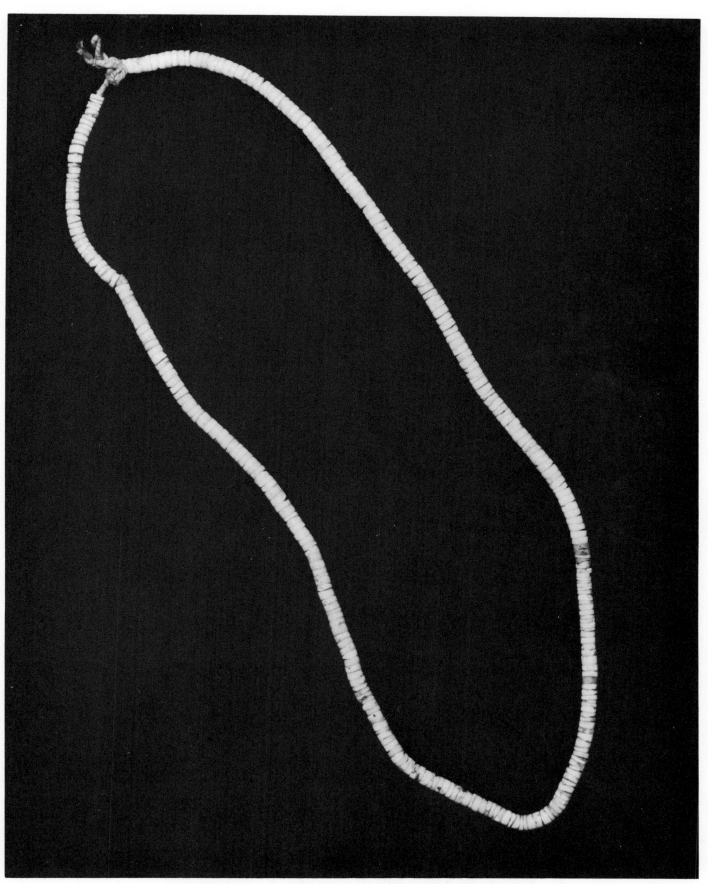

Round discs of wampum were painstakingly carved down to tiny beads and strung on sinew. These necklaces were precious ornaments to Northeastern Indians before the arrival of white traders with bright metal trinkets and pieces of silver.

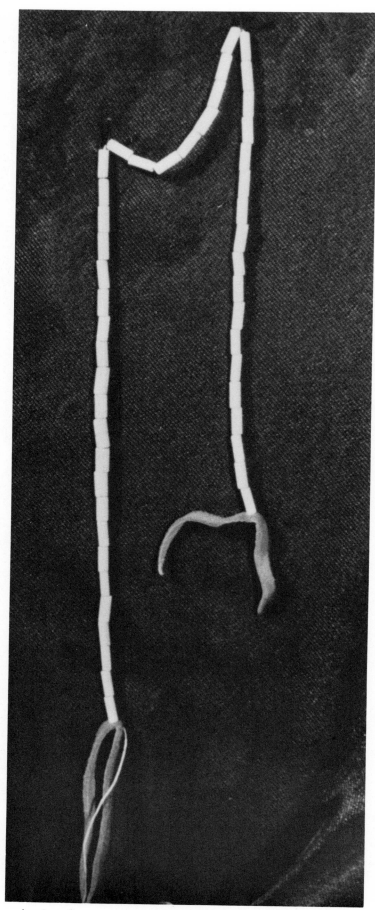

A string of wampum. COURTESY OF THE HODENOSHANEE COUNCIL
OF THE ARTS.

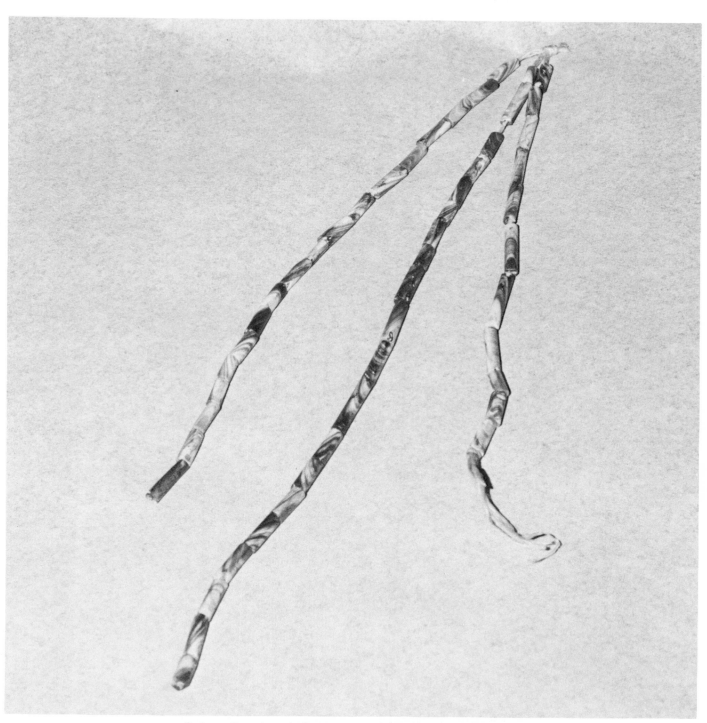

Strings of purple and white wampum dating from about 1700 tied together at the top.

parties. Its use spread all along the eastern seaboard through the seventeenth and first half of the eighteenth centuries. Commercial factories sprang up along the seacoast where conch shells were easy to obtain, since they were used as ballast in arriving ships. Wampum was also manufactured in Europe for export to America and the Indian trade agents. The abundance of it depreciated its value. But it seemed to sustain both Indians' and white settlers' need for currency. Three black plus six white wampum shells became equal to a penny. For the Indians, wampum now became both sacred and secular. They continued to use it in treaty belts, which contained pictographs designed in pink and white shells. Belts of black (really deep, deep purple) and white were used for political purposes. Speeches and tribal legends were recorded; invitation belts worn around runners' waists were sent to far away villages; and condolence wampum was made to lament the dead. No chiefs' meetings with whites were considered official unless the sacred council wampum was brought forth and displayed. A single string could be six inches long, and an elaborate belt of six feet might have up to a thousand intricately strung shells. Because wampum had become a feature of the economy of the era, it came as no surprise that a wampum mint was established in 1770 to produce commercial wampum for fur traders to buy.

The Campbell Brothers of Pascack, New Jersey (now Park Ridge), turned their machines to the manufacture of this product. This family-operated business thrived for five generations, until 1899, because wampum had followed white traders' thrust into Indian country in the West and was used out there in the fur trade.

The fact is that there was sacred wampum and there was commercial wampum —a lot of it —but it was fragile. Bits and pieces of strings that would hardly catch the eye might be spotted but not recognized for what it was. Only an expert and the use of X ray to determine if the holes were machine bored, could tell real from commercial wampum. Both are really rare at this time and equally valuable.

It's thought that a lot of people unknowingly own some of this very ordinary looking treasure.

13
MUSIC

MUSIC is still considered the pulse of true Indian culture. Unfortunately, television and movies have caused people to think only in terms of one dance —the war dance. There were hundreds of interpretive dances that created a universal language among Indian nations throughout America.

"There was a bond among Indians of all nations. Our ancestors could travel from nation to nation anywhere in red man's America and always find shelter and food. They would automatically be welcomed into the dance circle," said a Seneca dancing teacher. "The reason they could join in the dances is that rhythms were all taken from nature. Think of it; the wind in trees, a bird in flight, a clap of thunder, or bolt of lightning, the ripple of a creek on a quiet evening, the roar of waterfalls, or perhaps the sounds of animals that once echoed from dense forests. All of these sounds and motions speak of our music that revered nature. Dances were never suggestive or erotic, never ungraceful."

Drums, rattles, and beaters carried the rhythm for dances and songs that were chanted. Originally, instruments were constructed of materials taken symbolically from nature. The turtle shell, gourd, horn, hickory, elm bark, animal skin, and bird feather were all used to express musically the Woodlanders' appreciation of nature and its forces.

Dance titles included such names as The Great Feather Dance, False Face Dance, Bear, Eagle, Buffalo, and other animals. Many dances were used in False Face medicine ceremonies performed by the secret societies. Others were done by special dance groups at agricultural festivals, social gatherings, and adoption ceremonies. There were also dances at which all men, women, and children formed a circle and danced around the musicians and singers.

Over the years, music became subject to influences of the white man's culture. After all, it was easier to fashion a drum from a nail keg or wooden box than from a tree. Even tin cans were adapted and commercially tanned hides replaced woodchuck skins for drum tops.

"Indians were amazing in their ability to convert any materials to their craft use," said one collector. "It went along with their upbringing to use any and all

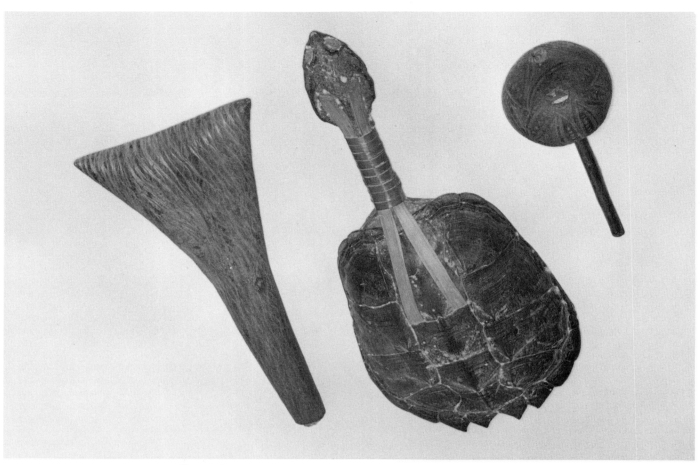

Pictured left to right are elm bark, turtle, and gourd rattles traditionally used in Iroquoian dances. COURTESY OF THE POP WARNER COLLECTION.

Gourd rattle incised with intricate designs. COURTESY OF THE POP WARNER COLLECTION.

This gourd rattle was made of a whole gourd with the neck cut off and a wooden handle substituted. COURTESY OF THE NEUMANN COLLECTION.

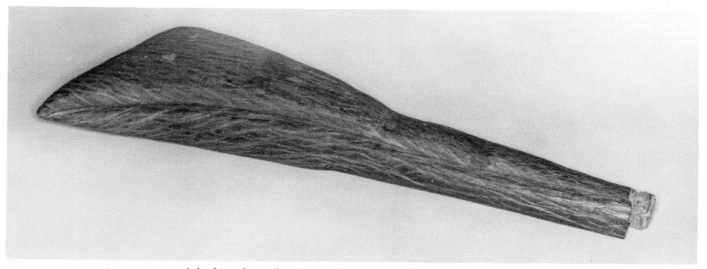

A bark rattle made of a single piece of bark folded over so that one-half fitted into the other to seal it. Kernels of corn were put inside and a plug sealed the end. COURTESY OF THE POP WARNER COLLECTION.

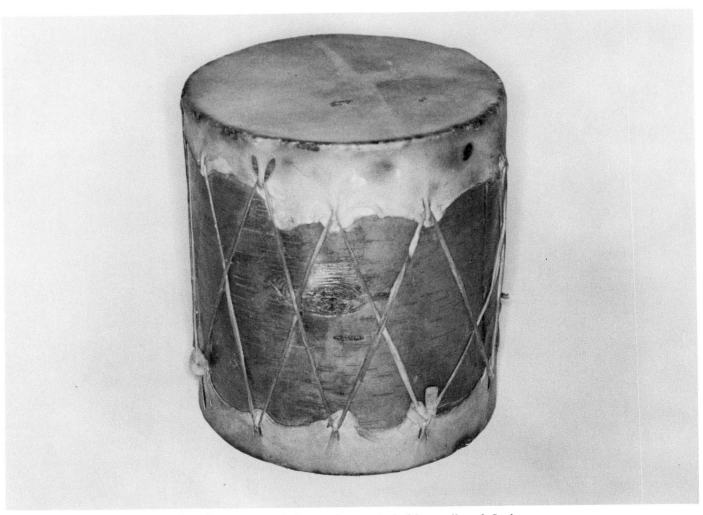

Late Reservation period water drum typical of those collected. Such items are selling as antiques today for forty-five to one hundred dollars. COURTESY OF THE NEUMANN COLLECTION.

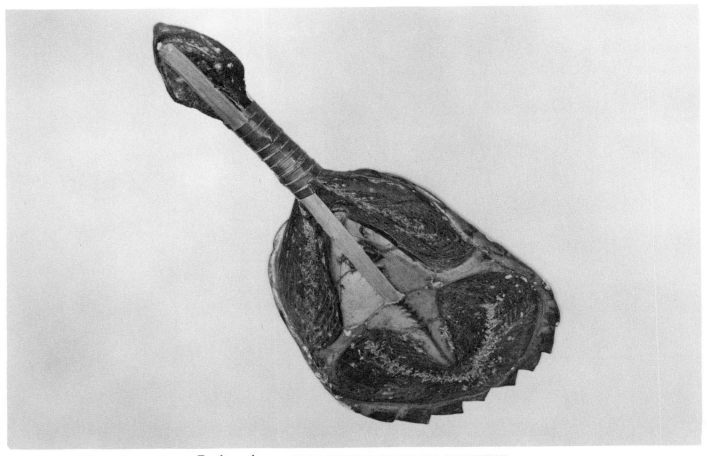

Turtle rattle. COURTESY OF THE POP WARNER COLLECTION.

materials that were available. You can't think that when an Indian wanted to make a water drum he was going to set out looking for a six-inch-round basswood tree when he had a nice little nail keg sitting next to his cabin! And you can't imagine that he would patiently burn out the center of the drum with red hot coals (from the fire) when he now owned a sharp chisel."

All sizes and shapes of old drums and rattles are attributed to Northeastern Indians. Many of them are not truly representative of anything except perhaps the Reservation period; however, the designs reveal Woodland origin. The turtle rattle and water drum, still being made today, are of Iroquoian origin. The rattle was made by removing the legs, tail and innards of a snapping turtle and then stretching the dried neck and head over a corn stalk or short stick and filling the cavity with a handful of flint, corn, or cherry stones. The opening was sewed up and the rattle was ready for use by a singer who straddled a log bench to sit and beat the rhythm by striking the edge of the turtle rattle shell against the log. Turtle rattles having many different tones would be used in the same dance.

The water drum was small, about eight inches across, and was held in one palm while being tapped with a stick in the other hand. It was water tight and the small amount of water in the bottom gave it a soft, vibrant tone. Before playing, the drummer would tip the drum upside down to moisten evenly the skin on top. The tap stick was held between two fingers and used lightly on the drum. Tap sticks could be ornately carved or very plain depending on the maker. Horn and bone rattles are interesting because of the various ways in which they were made.

In order to truly appreciate Indian music, dance, and costume, one must witness a culturally authentic Indian event. Only by actually hearing the sounds of nature symbolically reproduced can one experience the aesthetics of Woodland Indian music.

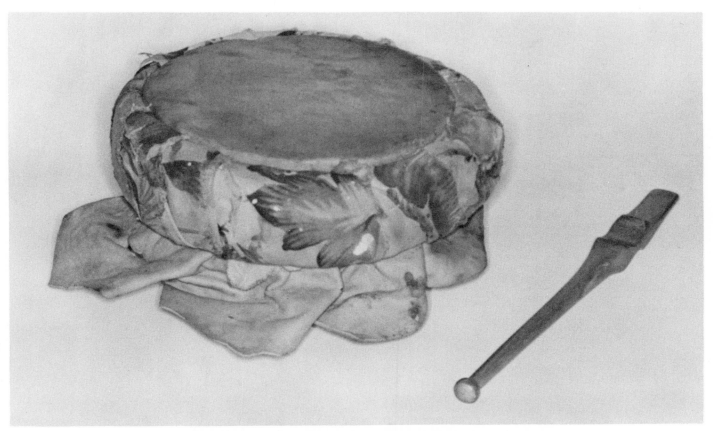

Iroquoian water drum. COURTESY OF THE NEUMANN COLLECTION.

Bottom of a water drum, showing how a small whiskey keg (note plug) was cut to about five inches in height to adapt it to an Indian's use. COURTESY OF THE NEUMANN COLLECTION.

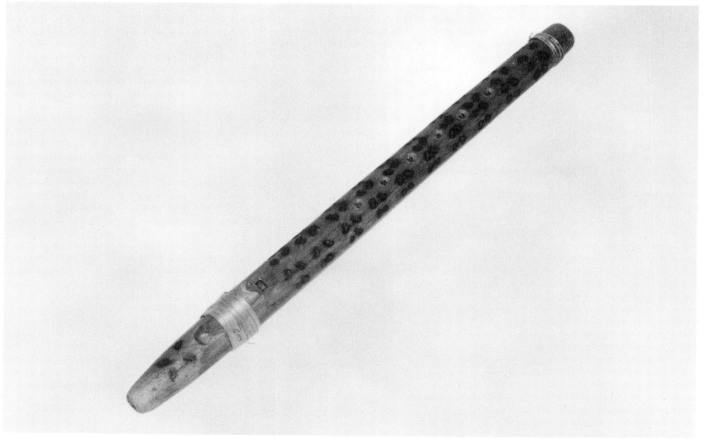

Carved flutes, called flagelots, were the only wind instruments native to the Northeast. They are often labeled as courting flutes. These instruments had little to do with ceremonies and were mostly for personal enjoyment.

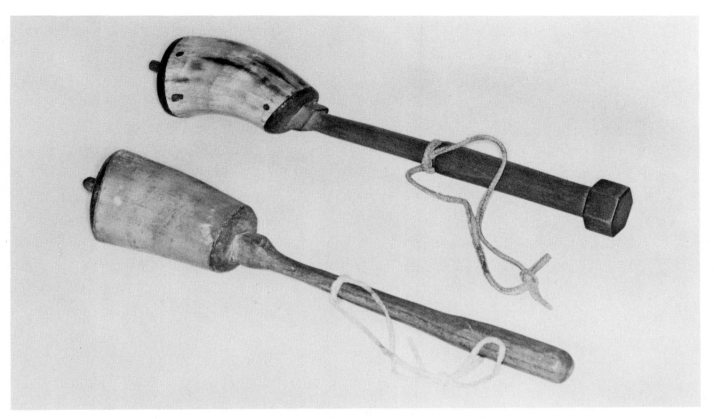

These are cow-horn rattles of the late Reservation period. Rattles of many varieties and sizes were made from horns that were scraped thin, filled with seeds or tiny pebbles, and had a wooden handle inserted. COURTESY OF THE NEUMANN COLLECTION.

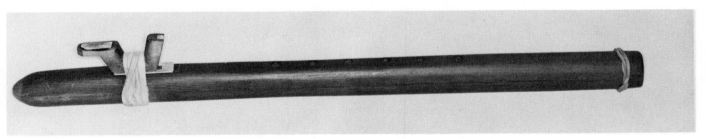

Flutes revealed many styles of workmanship and design and were very much sought by collectors during the Reservation period. COURTESY OF THE NEUMANN COLLECTION.

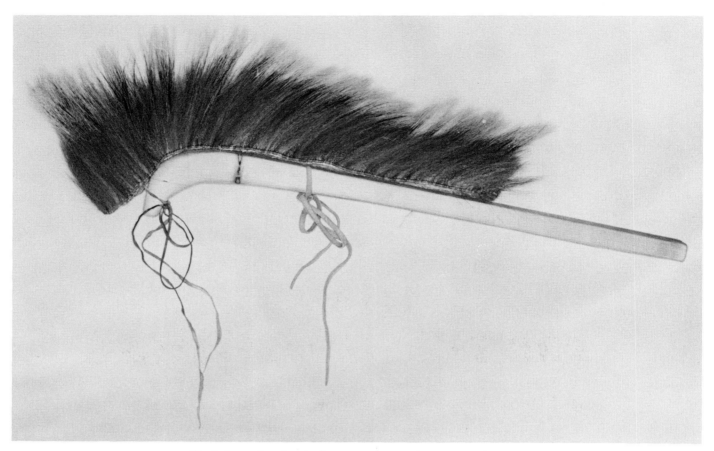

The hair roach, a head adornment worn for dances, is said to have originated with Eastern Indians. This one is tied on a wooden frame to keep its shape. COURTESY OF THE NEUMANN COLLECTION.

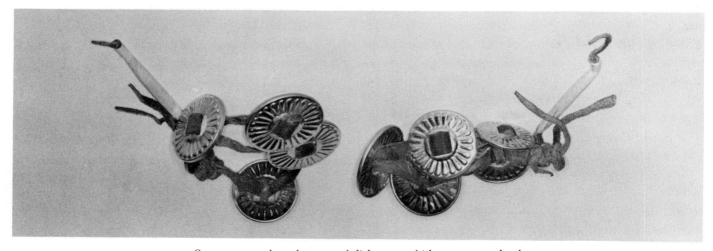

Ornaments such as these metal disks on rawhide were created to be worn on the upper arms or around the ankles. They dressed up the dance routine, often clinking together as the dancer moved. COURTESY OF THE NEUMANN COLLECTION.

14

PRINTS AND PAINTINGS

YOU can find paintings and prints of Northeastern Indians if you know your subject matter. A working familiarity with Woodland Indian tribe names, their bead designs, headdress styles, and silver ornamentations could pay big dividends when you least expect it. Recently one informed collector knew enough to bid on an oil portrait of Red Jacket at a household auction. The portrait turned out to have been done from life. Another collector, just six months ago, purchased three lithographs, one of Cornplanter and two of Western Indians. She expects to trade with a Western Indian enthusiast through want ads in antique collectors' newspapers.

The kinds of works available to collectors today are paintings and prints of Indians by artists of the eighteenth and nineteenth centuries who were fascinated by "the noble savage" as he was often described. They recorded, on canvas, the details of Indian clothing and scenes from real life in their villages.

Early Indians didn't actually do paintings as such. Their artwork was evidenced on their craft designs and such objects as ceremonial wooden utensils, condolence canes, drum heads, stone carvings, and pictographs. A few of these rare and fragile pictographs on bark are in museums and private collections. Seldom, if ever, do they turn up in antique shops or at auctions.

Among the great masterpieces that hang in museums and galleries are paintings depicting Northeastern Indians that were done just before and during the American revolution period by George Romney, Benjamin West, Charles W. Peale, and John Vanderlyn. These elaborate paintings were more concerned with composition and style than with exact details of Indians and their true dress. Other oils were only available for the enjoyment of the very rich. Early in the 1800s, however, all of this changed with the invention of lithography. A new trend was launched. For the first time, people of ordinary means were able to enjoy reproductions of art in their homes. Prints depicting America's history and landscapes were very popular. Indian subjects were particularly sought and artists rushed to record true-life scenes of these vanishing

A lucky family discovered this painting of Red Jacket stowed away and forgotten. Notes on the back of the watercolor and on the piece of wood that held it in the old frame add greatly to the value of this antique.

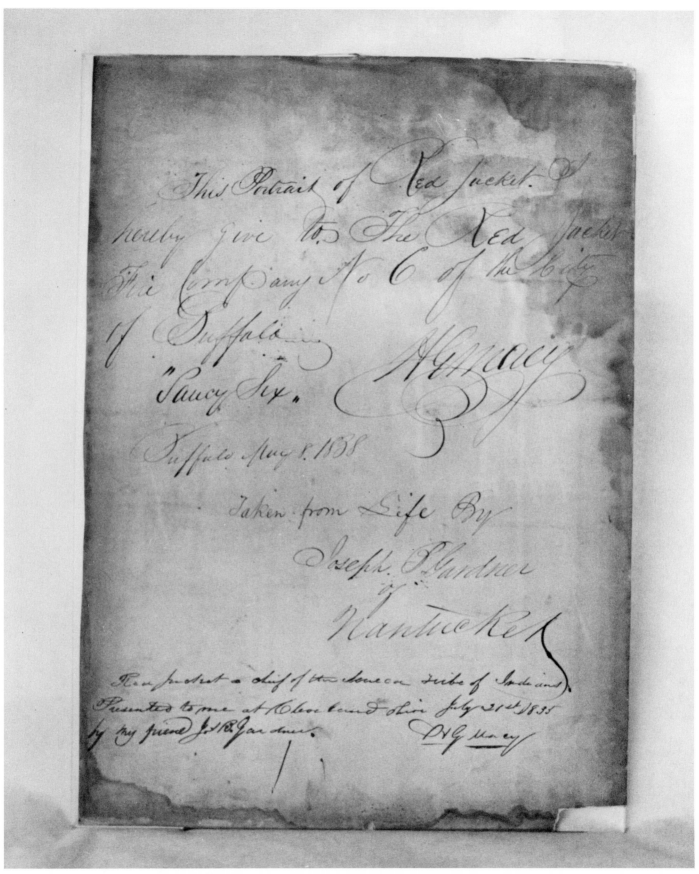

*Reverse side of the watercolor of Red Jacket has a note saying that
it was taken from life by Joseph B. Gardner of Nantucket and given
by the artist to Henry Macy in 1835 at Cleveland, Ohio.*

*The back piece of the Red Jacket watercolor frame completes the
story and demonstrates how Northeastern Indian antiques turn up
unexpectedly. Mr. Macy obviously kept the painting for fifty years
before giving it to the Red Jacket Fire Company No. 6 in Buffalo,
New York, in the year 1888.*

Joseph Brant, a Mohawk Chief, was painted by George Romney as well as Benjamin West. The originals hang in the National Galleries in Ottawa and Washington and have been reproduced many times. Brant's loyalty to the British during the Revolutionary War caused them to give the Mohawk Indians lands on the Grand River, Ontario, Canada, now called Six Nations Reserve. This is a copy of an engraving by John R. Smith. FROM THE DICTIONARY OF AMERICAN PORTRAITS, DOVER PUBLICATIONS, INC., 1967. COURTESY OF NEW YORK HISTORICAL SOCIETY.

Such scenes of grandeur were originally painted for gallery walls and were concerned with style, composition, and atmosphere. Benjamin West's famous painting of Willian Penn's Treaty was reproduced in prints to meet the decorating tastes of the Victorian period. COURTESY OF THE ALFRED DAVISON COLLECTION.

TRADING WITH INDIANS

Another artist's portrayal of the noble savage in an almost fairy-talelike setting. Formal studies such as these were followed by the era of on-the-scene action sketches and paintings of artists who went West and recorded buffalo hunts, war dances, and tepee villages. COURTESY OF THE ALFRED DAVISON COLLECTION.

[137]

KI-ON-TWOG-KY or CORN PLANT

A SENECA CHIEF.

PUBLISHED BY E. C. BIDDLE, PHILADELPHIA.

Cornplanter, a Seneca Chief, was one of the Government Indian
Portrait Gallery canvases reproduced in the McKenny & Hall
works. This lithograph, published by E. C. Biddle, Philadelphia,
1837, is typical of the way in which chiefs were portrayed. The print
sold for eighty dollars in 1973.

Americans. Many of those artists speculated on reproducing their works in printed portfolio collections. Others allowed their paintings to be used for prints in books and collected works that have since found their way to rare-book auctions.

Thomas McKenney, who was the Superintendent of Indian Trade from 1816 to 1822, sincerely believed that Indians were about to become extinct. He pleaded with Congress to begin a collection of Indian portraits. He told them that he was concerned over "the expediency of preserving the likenesses of some of the most distinguished among the most extraordinary race of people."[1] He asked them to invest two hundred dollars to begin such a project, but it was several years before his pleas were answered and the government finally agreed to begin gathering likenesses of Indians. The fee was about thirty-three dollars per portrait. They were intended to convey forever to posterity, "What sort of a being was the red man of America?" Portrayed in modified Indian dress with silver ornaments and a placid look on their faces, the paintings were intended to become symbols of a harmonious future for Indians and whites. One hundred sixteen heads were initially done for the Indian Portrait Gallery collection. Charles B. King, A. Ford, S. M. Charles, G. Cooke, Shaw, and an artist who initialed his paintings R. T. were among those who first sold portraits of Indian chiefs to the government.

McKenney chose Charles Bird King as the official artist for the government's Portrait Gallery work. King, who had studied in London under the master Benjamin West, was an accepted artist with a studio in Washington. Chiefs in Indian delegations who visited Washington came to his studio for their sittings. By that time, many who came were Western Indians, which makes an Eastern Indian portrait or litho a real find and very valuable. For inclusion in the gallery, King also copied selected works of other artists giving them all a 17½-by-14-inch format.

McKenney launched a second project in 1836. With the financial backing of James Hall, he organized the publication of *The McKenney-Hall Portrait Gallery of American Indians*, using the government collection as its basis. An artist named Henry Inman was commissioned to copy the original collection so that it could be lithographed on stone. It was to be issued in three huge volumes containing one hundred twenty portraits. Volume I was published in Philadelphia by Key & Biddle in 1836 and reissued by them the next year. Volume II was published in 1838 by Frederick W. Greenough (Biddle's successor), who also reissued Volume I at that time. Volume III appeared in 1844 with the names Daniel Rice and James G. Clark as publishers, and they also reissued Volumes I and II. The McKenney-Hall volumes continued to be reprinted in various sizes until almost 1865. Original published sets that were once offered for $120 today would bring $1,000 or more per volume if they happened to appear at auction. Complete volumes are mostly limited to rare-book sections in public libraries. However, over the years, individual prints were removed from numerous volumes for framing or sale. It is these lithos that appear, from time to time, on the art market. When one collector can tell another that he has just acquired an old McKenney-Hall print, it's great news.

For almost thirty-five years after its inception in 1822, the Government Indian Portrait Gallery grew and was exhibited many times. As McKenney had envisioned, the collection was "a grouping of our Indians from the four corners of our land, as an affair of great interest, and which posterity will be thankful for."[2] The collection was moved to the Smithsonian Institution in 1858. Other artists came to Washington to try to sell their works to the Smithsonian collection. John Mix Stanley offered 150 canvasses, then appraised at twenty thousand dollars. Congress refused him even a hundred dollars a year to meet interest on his debts in return for his paintings. He left his works at the Smithsonian in hopes of an eventual sale. In all, the Smithsonian collections grew to 350 paintings which were irreplaceable. A final tragic event culminated years of personal and financial frustrations for McKenney as well as the artists involved. The entire collection in the Government Indian Portrait Gallery (with the exception of a few of Stanley's and King's works that were out on display) was destroyed by the Smithsonian fire in 1865. Both McKenney and King had died by this time, so they never knew the outcome of their efforts. Stanley, of course, was devastated. He did one last great canvas, *The Trial of Red Jacket*. It took him three years to complete a six-

[1] F. W. Hodge. *The Origin and Destruction of a National Indian Portrait Gallery* (Bureau of American Ethnology, Holmes Anniversary Volume, p. 190). Washington D.C.: 1916.

[2] Hodge, p. 191.

Chromolithograph of John Mix Stanley's Trial of Red Jacket. *Chief Red Jacket, in the center, is defending himself against the charge of sorcery made by Handsome Lake (standing on the left) and Cornplanter (seated on the right). These two-by-three-foot chromolithographs are currently selling from three hundred to five hundred dollars.*

by-nine-foot canvas that is now housed at the Buffalo & Erie County New York Historical Society. It contains seventy-two authentically costumed Indians. Each one is a portrait, and the canvas is considered one of the greatest existing paintings of Iroquois Indians because Stanley knew these Indians and had seen Red Jacket many times. The painting was not done from life, but records a scene said to have occurred in 1803.

The Inman originals that were done for the McKenney-Hall lithos eventually made their way to the Peabody Museum in Cambridge, Massachusetts. Charles King had duplicated sixteen of his works done for the McKenney-Hall production and bequeathed them to the Redwood Library in Newport, Rhode Island, his hometown.

There were other artists competing for sales of their Indian artwork during this same period. George Catlin was one of them. He once wrote, "I have brought home safe and in good order, 310 oil portraits and 200 other paintings."[3] His earliest known painting is an unfinished portrait of Red Jacket, signed and dated 1826. Although he painted a few Woodland Indians, Catlin wasn't interested in civilized Indians who lived in log houses with stone fireplaces and wore suits and dresses. He went on to the West.

Examples of early-1800 books that included prints of Woodland Indian subjects were: *Sketches of a Tour to The Great Lakes* (1827) with twenty-nine engravings from paintings by James O. Lewis; *The First Aboriginal*

[3] George Catlin. *Illustrations of the Manners, Customs and Conditions of North American Indians.* London: Henry Bohn, 1851, p. 1.

A pair of prints, dating about 1860, were done in England by artists who used textbook descriptions to depict Indians in faraway America as romantic and exotic. The six-by-nine-inch prints, referred to as EUROPEAN IMPRESSIONS, sold for nine dollars each at an antique show in New York City in early 1974.

RECEPTION OF A NARRAGANSETT WARRIOR BY WINTHROP.

LAMBERVILLE SENT AWAY BY THE ONONDAGAS.

FIRST SETTLEMENT OF NEW YORK.

Old prints like this one are popular in the current Americana craze.
The artist put Western feathers on the Indians, which suggests that
he painted from his mind's eye rather than from accurate research.
COURTESY OF THE ALFRED DAVISON COLLECTION.

A collector who knows that St. Regis was a Northeastern Indian village would spot this print among the pages of a very old book and have a fine acquisition. COURTESY OF THE ALFRED DAVISON COLLECTION.

Port-Folio (1835), in three volumes with seventy-two illustrations by James O. Lewis; *Illustrations of the Manners, Customs and Conditions of North American Indians* (1851) by Catlin with three hundred sixty engravings from the author's original works, published when the author lived in London: and *Among the Great Masters of Oratory* (1901) by Rowlands with the reproduction of J. M. Stanley's chromolithograph *The Trial of Red Jacket*.

From time to time, complete volumes of such books must have passed through auction marts, booksellers' shops, and antique dealers' hands. But in all likelihood, a rare-book dealer can no longer provide you with any complete copies of these titles. Precious prints have long been separated from such old books and sold and resold over the decades. It's the challenge of finding prints in other early editions of texts, histories, geographies, and trips or tours that spurs us on!

15

COLLECTIBLES

THE subject of Indians has always been a fascinating and newsworthy one presented in many ways. To the collector, an artifact represents a specific historic object such as a mask or arrowhead that was made by an Indian. It predates an antique, which may have been made by the Indian (corn-husk dolls) or specifically for him (trade silver) and is at least seventy-five years old. Collectibles are not as old as antiques and are a category of the miscellaneous items that tell more about the subject but are not really a part of it —for example, glass lantern slides.

Indian portraits on old promotional merchandise such as mugs, souvenir plates, trays, teaspoons, buttons, nickels, badges, and even cigar-store Indians are still another complete collecting category. They aren't discussed in this book because they do not relate directly to the lives and antiquities of Indian family histories.

People who become caught up in Indian collections share several common bonds —not just a new appreciation for nature and its symbols, but an involvement

far beyond the objects themselves. This involvement is in the lives, emotions, and sadness of a bygone culture. Lifetime collectors have their bookshelves, desk drawers, and spare rooms jammed with collectibles that tell more of the story.

For instance, a condolence cane was carved by a Cayuga Indian for a lifelong white friend. As he twisted the cane to show the intricate carving, the old timer recalled how the Indian, in his late years, had regarded him as worthy, at last, of appreciating such a gift.

A note reading, "Indian beads plowed up by my grandfather," always has been attached to a tin box of very old glass beads owned by a farm woman. Farm families whose homes rest on lands once belonging to Indians frequently have such treasures around the house.

Another family owns a brass telescope with a note from a great-grandmother who recalled using it, in the early 1800s, to look down the country road. With it she could see Indians approaching the farm to ask for

This box, designed and made by a Shaker, was a wedding gift for an Indian bride.

Glass lantern slides are valuable antiques no matter what the subject, but when you come across some that were done on the travels of a student among Indians of the East and West in the early 1900s, you have an exciting acquisition.

*A chief's cane with notches that represent each of the fifty chiefs of
the Iroquois Nation.*

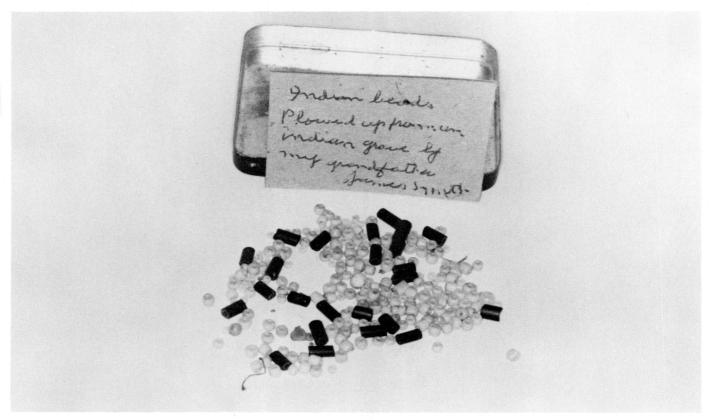

Indian beads plowed up on a farm in 1874. COURTESY OF MRS.
BERNICE C. REES.

work, either chopping wood or doing chores.

Old scrapbooks found at flea markets and antique shows often have newspaper clippings about Indian activities, obituaries of chiefs, and news pictures of gatherings and reservation pow wows in the early 1900s. Early editions of old books are fascinating in style and descriptions. Such passages as, "there was in the countenances of these half-caste Indian maidens a painful, wounded yet disdainful look that was very touching . . . " describe on-the-scene reactions of people to people.

Gifts of Indians to white friends reflect a definite two-way relationship that once existed.

"Why my ancestors gave everything away is beyond me," said a Seneca woman, "but I do know that Indians were far more generous than gullible. If an outsider came to his home and admired something, our grandfathers would just give it to him."

With every acquisition of an Indian artifact or antique comes a touch of someone's spirit that speaks quietly of both the magnificence and the heartbreak of an entire race of people.

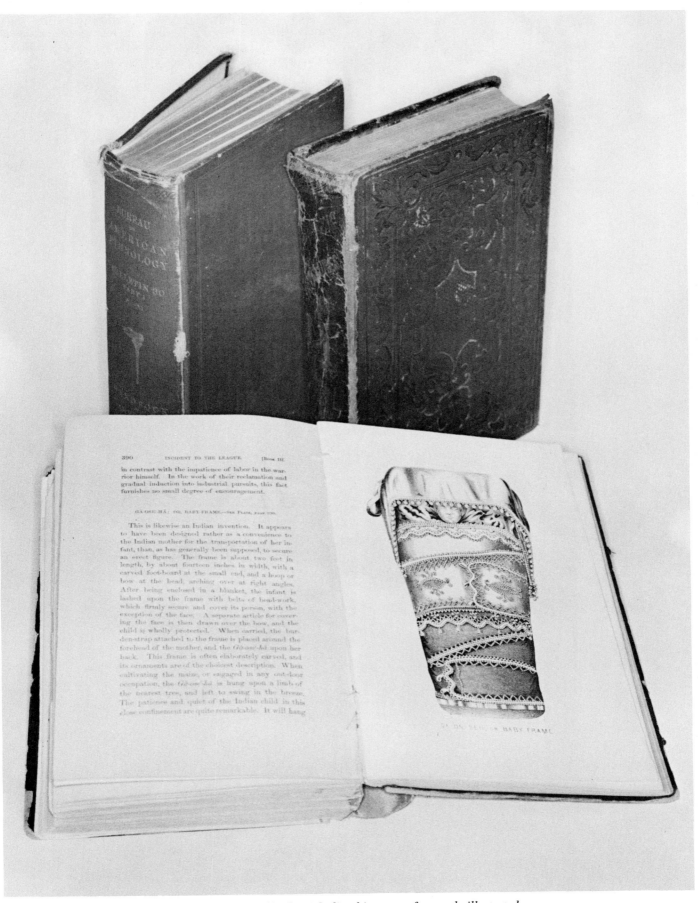

Early editions of books on Indian history are frequently illustrated with fine colored plates of drawings done on travels. This book is particularly desirable. It is the well-known LEAGUE OF THE IROQUOIS, by L. H. Morgan, 1851. The book was printed in two volumes and has been reprinted.

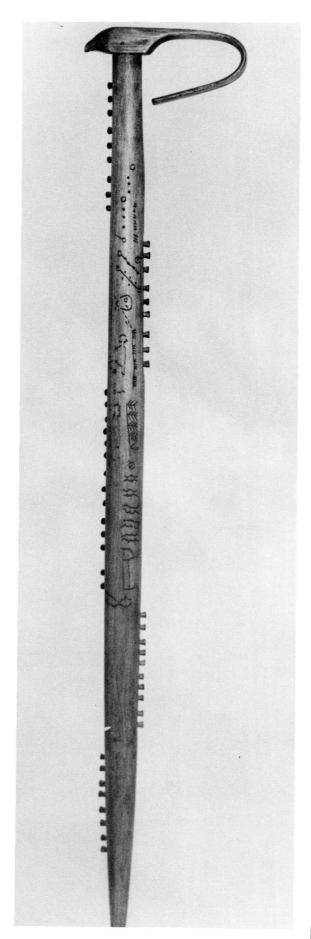

Condolence canes were used during the installation of a chief and at the death of a Sachem. They are highly valued and lavishly decorated. This one, an exact duplicate of the Cayuga condolence cane, was carved by an Indian as a gift to a friend.

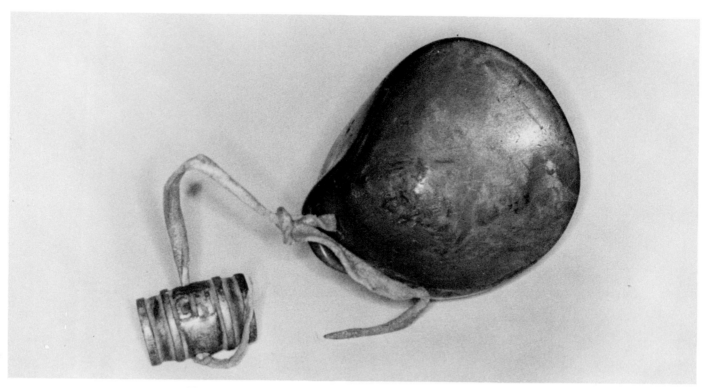

This drinking cup was made from half of a gourd. The strip of leather and wood plug enable the user to hook the cup through his belt. The owner made this cup for himself just as Indians made theirs. The memorable thing about the cup is that the owner used it on hunting, fishing, and camping trips during his long years of friendship and association with Indians. COURTESY OF THE NEUMANN COLLECTION.

BIBLIOGRAPHY

Background Reading

Bjorklund, Karna L. *Indians of Northeastern America*. New York: Dodd, Mead & Co., 1969.

Burland, Cottie. *North American Indian Mythology*. Middlesex, England: Hamlyn Publishing Group Ltd., 1968.

Colden, Cadwallader. *History of The Five Indian Nations*. Ithaca: Cornell Univ. Press, 1958.

Drumm, Judith. "Iroquois Culture." *State Ed. Dept. Leaflet No. 5*, Albany, N. Y.

Josephy, Alvin M., Editor. *The American Heritage Book of Indians*. New York: Simon & Schuster, 1961.

LaFarge, Oliver. *A Pictorial History of The American Indian*. New York: Crown Publishers, 1965.

Morgan, Lewis H. *The League of The Iroquois*. 2 vols. 1901. Reprint, 2 vols. New Haven: Yale Univ. Press, 1954.

Scherer, J. C. & Walker, J. B. *Indians*. New York: Crown Publishers, 1973.

Speck, Frank G. "The Iroquois." *Cranbrook Institute*: Bull. 23: Bloomfield Hills, Mich., 1945.

Underhill, Ruth. *Red Man's America*. Chicago: University Press, 1956.

Wallace, A. F. C. *Death & Rebirth of the Senecas*. New York: A. P. Knopf, 1970.

Wallace, Paul A. W. *Indians in Pennsylvania*. Harrisburg, Pa.: Pennsylvania Historical Society & Museum Commission, 1968.

Whiteford, A. H. *North American Indian Arts*. Racine, Wis.: Western Publishing, 1970.

Subject Reading

Appleton, L. H. *American Indian Design and Decoration*. New York: Dover Publications, 1971.

Beaucamp, Wm. M. *Metallic Ornaments of N. Y. Indians*. 1903 Reprint, Buffalo Enterprises, East Berlin, Pa.

Carter, W. H. *North American Indian Trade Silver*. Vols. 1 & 2. London, Ontario: W. H. Carter, 1971.

Edmonds, Walter D. *The Muskat and the Cross*. Boston: Little, Brown & Co., 1968.

Ewers, John Canfield. "Charles Bird King, Painter of Indian Visitors to the Nations Capitol." *Smithsonian Institution Annual Report, 1953*. Wash., D. C.: (463–473).

Felder, Norman. *American Indian Art*. New York: H. N. Abrams, Inc., 1965.

Fenton, William N. "Masked Medicine Societies of The Iroquois." *Smithsonian Institution Annual Report 14, 1940*. Wash. D. C.

Horan, James D. *The McKenny-Hall Portrait Gallery of American Indians*. New York: Crown Publishers, 1972.

Langdon, John E. *Canadian Silversmiths, 1700–1900*. Toronto: Stienhour Press, 1966.

Lyford, Carrie. *Iroquois Crafts*. U. S. Dept. of Interior, Bureau of Indian Affairs, Washington, D. C., 1945.

Mason, Bernard S. *Book of Indian Crafts and Costumes*. South Brunswick and New York: A. S. Barnes and Co., 1946.

Miles, Charles W. *Indian & Eskimo Artifacts of North America*. New York: Bonanza Books, 1953.

Museum of the American Indian, Heye Foundation. *Beads and*

Beadwork of American Indians. New York, 1929.

Orchard, Wm. C. "Techniques of Porcupine-Quill Decorations Among North American Indians." *Museum of the American Indian, Heye Foundation* vol. 14, no. 1, 1916.

Parker, Arthur C. *The Indian How Book*. Garden City, N. Y.: Doubleday, 1937.

————. "Secret Medicine Societies of The Seneca." *American Anthropologist* vol 11, 1909.

Quimby, George I. *Indian Culture & European Trade Goods*. Madison, Wisconsin: University of Wisconsin Press, 1966.

Russell, Carl P. *Guns on the Early Frontiers*. Berkley: Univ. of Calif. Press, 1957.

Ritchie, Wm. A. *Typology & Nomenclature for N. Y. Projectile Points*. Albany: State Dept of Education, bull. 384, 1961.

Museums with Northeastern Woodland Indian Collections

American Museum of Natural History, New York City
Brooklyn Museum, Brooklyn, N. Y.
Buffalo & Erie County Historical Society, Buffalo, N. Y.
Buffalo Museum of Science, Buffalo, N. Y.
Chicago Natural History Museum, Chicago, Ill.
Museum of the American Indian, Heye Foundation, New York City
National Museum of Canada, Ottawa
Newark Museum, Newark, N. J.
New York State Museum, Albany, N. Y.
Peabody Museum, Harvard Univ., Cambridge, Mass.
Rochester Museum of Arts & Sciences, Rochester, N. Y.
Smithsonian Institution, Washington, D. C.
Univ. of Pennsylvania, Philadelphia
Woodland Indian Cultural Centre, Brantford, Canada

INDEX